CRIPPLE CREEK DISTRICT

DISTRICT

LAST OF COLORADO'S GOLD BOOMS

Because the district grew so quickly and changed so often, maps were often out of date within a short time. This map, from the Cripple Creek Sunday Herald, *was published in 1895 and shows several district towns. (Courtesy Cripple Creek District Museum.)*

THE
MAKING OF AMERICA
SERIES

CRIPPLE CREEK
DISTRICT
LAST OF COLORADO'S GOLD BOOMS

JAN MACKELL
CRIPPLE CREEK DISTRICT MUSEUM

ARCADIA
PUBLISHING

Published by Arcadia Publishing
Charleston, South Carolina

Printed in the United States of America

Library of Congress control number: 2002114935

For all general information contact Arcadia Publishing at:
Telephone 843-853-2070
Fax 843-853-0044
E-mail sales@arcadiapublishing.com
For customer service and orders:
Toll-Free 1-888-313-2665

Visit us on the Internet at www.arcadiapublishing.com

DEDICATION

This book is dedicated to each and every person who made the
Cripple Creek District what it was and what it is.

FRONT COVER: *A miscellaneous photograph of miners from the district shows their diversity. Note the African-American miner, a rare sight in a predominantly white industry. (Courtesy Cripple Creek District Museum.)*

CONTENTS

ACKNOWLEDGMENTS

The writing of this book would not have been possible without a number of people and organizations. First and foremost, the Cripple Creek District Museum has been an integral part of this project, providing roughly 90 percent of the photographs used herein. I am so thankful that museum benefactors and directors, such as Richard Johnson, Blevins Davis, Leland Feitz, and Erik Swanson, had the foresight to preserve everything they could get their hands on with determined dignity and grace. Without the museum, such very important documents, photographs, maps, letters, diaries, and books would be lost forever—or be up for sale on eBay.

A fair amount of credit also must go to Marshall Sprague. As the author of *Money Mountain*, as well as a number of other wonderful books about Colorado, Sprague continues to set precedence for recording the Cripple Creek District's incredible story. *Money Mountain* is considered by many as the "Bible" of the district's history. In this book, I have attempted to provide details that Sprague did not, rather than surpass the fine work he did. My hat is still off to him and I will be forever indebted to his spirit for providing a starting point for writers like myself.

Also, the following people and organizations were of immense help and inspiration not only during the writing of this book, but also in subsequent projects I have undertaken. They include, but are certainly not limited to, Dick Johnson, president of the board at the Cripple Creek District Museum; Erik Swanson, director of the Cripple Creek District Museum; Art and Loretta Tremayne; Margaret and June Hack; Harold and Lodi Hern; Charlotte Bumgarner; Mary Davis at Penrose Library in Colorado Springs; Encore Videos; Stephanie Hilliard; Georganna and Bud Peiffer; Mary Sanders; Ohrt Yeager; Mike Moore; the Denver Public Library; the Internet Goddess; all the helpful folks at Cripple Creek and Victor City Halls; the Teller and El Paso County Courthouses; and every other library within a 300-mile radius of my home.

In retrospect, I would also like to thank the people who inspired me most in my writing. They include Eleanor Smith, my mother, mentor, and best friend; Jimmy, Victor, Dawn, and Tricia for reminding me to be young and think freely; my dad, Wally Smith, for giving me business smarts and letting me do things against his better judgment; Irene Smith for asking me, "So, you want to be a writer?"; Buck Gibbons, my paramour, copy reader, and friend for life; Russ Williams for encouraging me to be myself; Tom Noel, Cathleen Norman, Linda Wommack, Sharon Sweeney, David Lichtenstein, Richard Marold, Larry Ferguson, and Kathy Kniss for being my associates in crime; and all of my rowdy friends who put up with my temperamental tendencies and understand what the word "deadline" means.

~ Jan MacKell

Cripple Creek was just a budding boomtown in 1893. Before long, the town and its namesake district would be known around the world. (Courtesy Cripple Creek District Museum.)

INTRODUCTION

Who would have thought that a cow pasture could yield millions of dollars in gold and spawn a city so large it rivaled Denver for the state capitol? Bob Womack did and it is his determination we have to thank for the historic Cripple Creek District we see today.

Upon arriving during the 1870s, Robert Miller Womack's family established a cattle ranch near what is today Cripple Creek. Wandering the hills daily, Bob's prior prospecting experience led to his discovery of gold. Womack's dream of a booming gold camp was finally realized in 1891. By 1893, the Cripple Creek District was in a constant state of progress with new construction, new stage roads, and a growing population. Telephones, telegraph lines, and even electricity had been installed, making Cripple Creek one of the first cities in the nation to have such modern amenities.

Within three years, Cripple Creek's population had grown to 10,000 residents. Several more camps, towns, and cities were springing up in the district. Passengers on the newly constructed Midland Terminal Railroad rolled into a typical frontier town at both Cripple Creek and Victor. Both towns were filled with wooden false-front buildings containing banks, mercantiles, saloons, churches, opera houses, schools, boarding houses, restaurants, mining and real estate offices, hardware and furniture stores, laundries, newsstands, drugstores, bakeries, brothels, and assay offices. Every imaginable business prospered in the district and the wise investor stood little chance of losing money.

Fire, an ever imposing threat on boom towns across the country, was inevitable in the Cripple Creek District. Of Cripple Creek's three early fires, two stand out as crucial turning points in the city's development. During a four-day period in April of 1896, two separate conflagrations nearly destroyed the town. In the aftermath of the first fire, over 3,600 people lost their homes and businesses as 15 acres went up in smoke. During the second blaze, all but two buildings on Bennett Avenue burned, as well as a good portion of the residential district. Thousands were homeless and sought shelter in makeshift tents and neighboring towns.

What could have been the demise of any other town was a mixed blessing for Cripple Creek. Within four years, a bigger, better city rose from the ashes. The town rebuilt in solid brick and the city lost its rough and shabby frontier town

The Anchoria Leland Mine was one of hundreds in Cripple Creek. Considered to be one of the best early producers in the district, the Anchoria Leland had its own assay office and milled over a million dollars in gold by 1900. (Courtesy Cripple Creek District Museum.)

look. A random stroll down any avenue revealed a city bustling with business. Here, one could purchase fine china at the May Company or the best meal in the state at the National Hotel. A number of saloons, gambling halls, dance halls, and parlor houses fairly seethed with life.

The district's second largest city, Victor, also suffered a fire in August of 1899. In its wake, residents of Cripple Creek and other nearby towns came to the rescue. This time, Frank and Harry Woods hired a variety of builders, including Denver architect Matthew Lockwood McBird. Within just a few months, Victor also rebuilt into a fine working-class city. By 1900, investors from around the world were flocking to the Cripple Creek District as mines produced more millions than anyone had imagined.

By the turn of the last century, the Cripple Creek District had become a household word not only across America, but all over the world. Everyone knew where Cripple Creek was and many yearned to seek their fortunes there. Among those celebrities hailing from the district were boxer Jack Dempsey, travel writer and radio personality Lowell Thomas, Colorado Governor Ralph Carr, and nightclub queen Texas Guinan. Famous visitors to the district included Theodore Roosevelt, Groucho Marx, Lily Langtree, and a number of musicians and movie stars.

Two labor wars occurred in the Cripple Creek District. The first, in 1893, settled in favor of the miners. The second labor war was much more violent. Riots and gunfights broke out as striking miners were deported by train to the state borders. There were deaths, injuries, and inhumane acts. At one point, a Gatling gun was temporarily installed in the middle of Bennett Avenue in Cripple Creek as a deterrent to violence. By the time the strikes were settled statewide in about 1907, the mines were thought to be playing out and people began leaving the district in search of greener pastures.

Thankfully, some of the pioneer families who called the district home for decades chose to stay, living in what was left of the district even as it decayed under their feet. Through both World War I and World War II, the cities and towns continued to shrink as buildings were dismantled for use in reconstruction or firewood. Others simply sank into the ground under the weight of winter snows and age. As a result, only three towns exist today: Cripple Creek, Victor, and the district's third largest city, Goldfield. Each are just about one-fifth of their original size. Roughly four ghost towns remain visible to the naked eye, with several others either completely gone or buried forever under mine tailings.

Beginning in the late 1940s and continuing into the 1980s, the district evolved into a quaint tourist destination. Then in about 1989, Cripple Creek and other towns like it began considering legalized gambling to save their historic integrity. A century after its birth, Cripple Creek's rebirth came in the form of limited stakes gaming. Alongside the gaming came the Cripple Creek and Victor Mine, which is currently the largest open pit mine in the state.

Today, 12 casinos line Bennett Avenue in Cripple Creek and the city is 10 years into its second boom in 100 years. The city of Victor is surviving as a non-gaming residential town with a healthy population, while Goldfield has melded into a quiet bedroom community with no commercial businesses. Live music, street festivals, and a series of other events take place regularly within the district. Many of them, such as Donkey Derby Days and Gold Rush Days, are traditions dating back as long as 70 years; others are new events spawned out of the need for tourism. True to its heritage, the Cripple Creek District continues to be a wonderful year-round destination for residents and visitors of all ages.

1. Before the District and How It Was Formed

The Cripple Creek District, known in its heyday as "The World's Greatest Gold Camp," lies on the backside of Pikes Peak in what is commonly known as a caldera, or the top of a deep volcano measuring roughly 24 square miles. The caldera is surrounded on all sides by a rough and crumbly combination of quartz, feldspar, and mica. At the edge of the caldera is what is today known as Mt. Pisgah. Over 35 million years ago, 10,400-foot Mt. Pisgah was another small volcano. When the larger volcano collapsed after erupting through older rock, giant boulders shattered around the basin. Later, more volcanic activity caused mineral-rich solutions, including gold, to flow into the faults and fissures created by the collapse. The veins cooled, condensed, and hardened over time.

"Geologically Cripple Creek is a freak," *The Chicago Times* would later report in 1896. "It is a vast crater bed in which the elements once were wont to make merry with nature and play unexpected pranks that must have caused the systematic old dame many a vexatious hour."

The amount of heat during this activity was unusually intense. The volcanic flow into the faults hardened over thousands of years. As uplifting took its toll, outcroppings of rich sylvanite, calverite, and gold made their way to the top of the earth's crust. Over still more years, the outcroppings were buried under granite, dirt, and rocks. Thus, the hidden treasures of the district sat, waiting until the day someone discovered them. But the first people to inhabit the area were not seeking gold. They were Ute Indians, who favored the high country meadows as an abundant hunting ground.

Historians have been unable to pinpoint exactly when the Ute tribes first came to Colorado or even where they migrated from. The Utes themselves simply say they have been here "since the beginning." It is thought that the Ute nation is descended from the Desert culture, the Fremont tribes, and perhaps even the Basket Makers, which would date their presence in Colorado to 10,000 years ago or more. Archaeological evidence suggests there were human inhabitants of the area more than 11,500 years ago. Other sources speculate the Utes may have migrated from Mexico, since their native tongue is deemed Uto-Aztecan. The

Manitou Springs went from serving as a sacred place for the Indians to a health resort in just a few short years. Even today, Manitou Springs strongly resembles its former self—the exception being lots more trees and foliage.

Ute language is similar to those of the Shoshone, Comanche, Bannock, Hopi, Chemehuevi, and Paiute tribes, all of whom the Utes consider relatives.

In the early eighteenth century, when Comanches first appeared in Colorado, the Utes helped them drive out the Apaches. As early as 1637, the Apaches had been living south of the Cripple Creek District close to the Arkansas River. By about the mid-1700s, however, the Utes and Comanches had become enemies. During that time, the Utes became friendly with the Jicarilla Apaches. The two tribes intermarried and adopted one another's children. The Utes remained friendly with both the Apache and Shoshone tribes, but were enemies with the Plains Native Americans and Navajo for many generations. Later, the Utes often traded and even married with both the Navajo and Pueblo Indians. Children of such unions, however, are generally referred to as Utes.

Largely due to their dislike for Plains Indians, the Ute tribes were hunters and gatherers. Rather than farming on prairie land, the Utes migrated closer to the mountains where there was an abundance of berries and wildlife to supply food. In the Pikes Peak region, Utes occupied the slopes around the peak for thousands of years. A favorite spot was at the entrance to an ancient pass at the base of Pikes Peak. The Utes commanded the mountainous regions of Colorado, guarding their Ute Pass and other sacred areas against imposing tribes. Ute outposts were still visible along the pass as late as 1920.

The Utes and other tribes also found one common sanctuary at what is now known as Manitou Springs. Located just west of Colorado Springs, Manitou's mineral springs were amazing to the Native Americans. Here, seemingly magical, bubbling springs flowed from massive underwater caverns. The Utes believed a great god, Manitou, resided below the springs. According to legend, Manitou's breathing gave the springs bubbles and steam, bringing health to all who drank from them.

To pay homage and establish their territory, the Utes made a yearly trek from their place high in the mountains to visit Manitou. Utes were adept at basketry, leather work, and sometimes undecorated clay wares, and they often left offerings of this nature, as well as beads and knives, around the natural springs. Such sacrifices also brought good hunting and luck in battles. The Utes had great faith in the springs' natural healing powers. Other tribes were permitted to pay homage as well, and Manitou was known as common ground among all nations. The area was treated as neutral territory by all tribes.

At the top of Ute Pass near Florissant, however, any immunity from war was forgotten. Battles with Arapaho, Comanche, and other tribes were common. The Ute's preference for the mountains included the area around the Cripple Creek District, which was used as a summer hunting ground. Because the district sits at an elevation close to 10,000 feet, however, the area did not make good winter quarters. Although the district actually receives less snow annually than many other parts of the state, nighttime temperatures in winter can dip below zero. The Utes accordingly spent their winters in the lower and warmer regions, such as northern New Mexico, once the snow began falling. Spring and fall were spent commuting and preparing for the alternate seasons.

The early town of Twin Creek was later renamed Florissant after a town in Missouri. Small from its inception, Florissant today is still a friendly community along State Highway 24. (Courtesy Cripple Creek District Museum.)

In 1763, the Treaty of Paris was signed in Europe giving all French claims to territory west of the Mississippi River to Spain. By this time, the Utes had befriended the Spanish, whom they initially regarded as enemies. A treaty between the two was established in 1675. Thus, when Father Atanasio Dominguez and Silvestre de Escalante traveled through Ute country looking for a passable road to California in 1776, the failure of their mission was countered with kind treatment by the Utes. By then, the Utes were accustomed to the presence of Spaniards, Mexicans, and eventually white settlers. They traded freely with early explorers in Colorado, as well as New Mexico and Arizona.

New Mexico Territorial Governor Don Juan Bautista de Anza was probably the first Spaniard to travel Ute Pass in August of 1779. De Anza was passing through in his quest to capture and kill Comanche leader Cuerno Verde (Spanish for Green Horn). His troops included about 600 Spanish soldiers, plus 200 Utes and Apaches. The arrogant young chief was destined to meet his end a month later, when de Anza's army killed him south of Pueblo. There was little other activity of note on Ute Pass for over two decades until November of 1806. That year, Zebulon Pike and a party of explorers traveled the pass and attempted to scale Pikes Peak. Upon discovering its actual height of 14,110 feet and width of 450 square miles, Pike deemed the peak unscalable and never climbed it.

In 1820, Major Stephen H. Long accomplished what Zebulon Pike could not. For a time, Pikes Peak was known as Longs Peak, prior to the latter name being assigned to a mountain near Estes Park to the north. Over the next several decades, more explorers and even a few fur-trappers braved the pass to observe its scenic

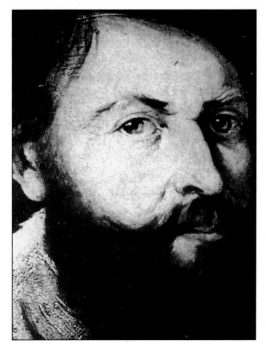

Juan Bautista de Anza, the first territorial governor of New Mexico, traveled extensively throughout Colorado during the 1700s. In 1779, de Anza traversed Ute Pass, roughly 18 miles from Cripple Creek, in pursuit of the Comanche leader Cuerno Verde.

wonders and partake of its bounty. Among them were Kit Carson, explorer John C. Fremont, and English adventurer George F. Ruxton, all of whom traversed Ute Pass during the 1840s. These men had the foresight to know that Ute Pass would some day serve as a highway for many travelers.

During the 1850s, the first reports of gold in Colorado were actually made by three Native Americans from the Delaware and Cherokee tribes who were on their way to the California goldfields. The two Cherokee men, called Lewis Ralston and John Beck, had already mined some in the east. A failure to strike it rich in California presumably led the men back to Colorado with a gold party. The other Native American, a Delaware known as Fall Leaf, returned to Kansas and showed his Colorado gold dust to a merchant in Lawrence. For some reason, however, Fall Leaf never came back to Colorado. The exact site of the men's claims remains a mystery.

The discovery by Ralston, Beck, and Fall Leaf coincided with the premonitions of Carson, Fremont, and Ruxton. The year 1859 saw the first use of Ute Pass by freighters. Hundreds of prospectors and merchants were making their way to the gold fields on the western slope of Colorado, often encountering angry Native Americans in their quests. Prospectors J.B. Kennedy, Dr. J.L. Shank, and D.M. Slaughter, the first men to stake claims in South Park, were later killed by Native Americans near Kenosha Pass. Despite such dangers, Augusta and Horace (H.A.W.) Tabor traversed the pass on their way to Leadville, where they struck it rich and made millions in the silver mines. The trip was indeed memorable for Augusta, who was ill and made the trek in a "sick wagon."

From all appearances, however, the Utes seemed to take the influx of newcomers in stride. Because of their passivity, the Utes have the distinction as one of the few tribes who were never officially conquered by another civilization. Although they often battled the Spanish in the early days, their leader Ouray eventually convinced his tribe to befriend the whites. Nevertheless, the Utes eventually lost their lands to the United States government and their way of life changed forever. Even today, there is very little documentation dedicated to their history.

Throughout the 1860s, Ute Pass became known as the "Gateway to the Goldfields." Those goldfields, however, were not destined to include the Cripple Creek District just yet. During the 1870s, the gold miners were preceded by ranchers who found the high plains soil to be very rich. Homesteaders in the Cripple Creek District included two important families who later became ingrained in the district's history forever: the Weltys and the Womacks.

The Welty family first made their appearance in the district in about 1871. The family migrated from a ranch near today's United States Air Force Academy that was in close proximity to the coming Denver & Rio Grande Railroad. Levi Welty disliked the railroad and the changes it was bringing, so the family migrated up Ute Pass. Accompanying Levi were three sons, Alonzo, Frank, and George. Initially, the men spent some time in the blossoming one-horse town of Twin Creek. Nearby, what are today known as the Florissant Fossil Beds had been attracting attention for some time. Cornell University student Theodore Meade

15

is recorded as the first person to observe and collect fossil specimens there in 1871. Over the next several years, other notable archaeologists would also visit the fossil beds, publishing numerous reports on the variety of specimens found there, before declaring the area a national monument.

At Twin Creek, the Weltys met Judge James Castello, who had established a trading post in 1870. Later, Castello changed the name of Twin Creek to Florissant after his hometown of Florissant, Missouri. On Castello's advice, Levi Welty and his family made their way towards what was then known as Pisgah Park and discovered some of the finest ranch land around. The four men erected a cabin near the stream they found running through the valley. Next, they built a shack over the stream to keep the wildlife from dirtying the water supply.

It was at this time, according to most historians, that Cripple Creek was named for a series of mishaps revolving around the little stream. Allegedly, one of the boys was injured by a falling log, Levi Welty suffered a flesh wound to his hand when his gun went off, and a calf or cow broke its leg crossing the stream. It is also said that visitors to the ranch may have suffered mishaps in the stream. In the aftermath, Levi Welty is said to have exclaimed, "Well, boys, this sure is some Cripple Creek!"

The story of the Welty's naming of Cripple Creek is plausible enough. It certainly seems more possible than the tale of the Civil War veteran whose lame leg was the namesake of the creek. Another account comes from an 1896 article in the *Quarterly Sentinel*. While admitting to confusion as to the origin of the name, the magazine offered yet another alternative:

> A second explanation runs to the effect that a little old house, still to be seen in Arequa, one of the numerous outlying camps, was occupied by a family from Posey County, Indiana, who were one day invited to a dance by some distant neighbors, originally from Arkansas, who happened to be passing. The Posey County lady answered that "We kain't go; all broke up; Sam's down with th' rumatiz; Betsy's got th' fever; Jake's got 'is arm broke; old Pied (the cow) broker 'er laig, and the hosses is run off . . . But if you all 'ill come over to Cripple Creek, we'll he'p ye out th' best we can fur yer hoedown."

In reality, however, Cripple Creek historian Leland Feitz offers a much more logical explanation. The year 1876 saw the arrival of the Womack family at Pisgah Park. The Womacks originally hailed from Kentucky, with deeper roots near a place that even today is still called Cripple Creek, Virginia. Feitz theorizes the creek was subsequently named for the Womack's homeland.

Samuel Womack and his wife Corella had four children. The oldest child, Robert Miller, was born in 1844. In 1861, Bob headed west from Kentucky with his father and the two took up mining in Colorado. Eventually, the rest of the family followed and, in 1876, the Womacks moved from their ranch near Colorado Springs to Cripple Creek. They purchased the Welty Ranch as Levi

This image shows old Broken Box Ranch, future site of Cripple Creek, as it appeared when the Weltys and the Womacks moved to the district. (Courtesy Cripple Creek District Museum.)

Welty moved his family west to the area known as Four Mile Creek. Bob built himself a shack on the Welty property, while his brother William moved into the ranch house with his wife Ida.

By then, Bob was a sometime cowboy with a bad case of gold fever. His appetite had already been whetted some three years before, when the United States Geological and Geographical Survey of the Territories arrived to chart the country west of Pikes Peak. Bob had readily supplied information about the terrain. A year later, a member of the survey team, H.T. Wood, came looking for Bob to tell him that he suspected there was gold in the area. In September of 1874, Bob Womack accompanied a group of nearly 100 prospectors to the Cripple Creek area. A 100-foot tunnel was blasted in what was later named Eclipse Gulch. The group optimistically christened the area the Mount Pisgah Mining District, but concluded that the chance of finding worthwhile gold deposits was only slight. Then they left, leaving Bob Womack with his own hopes and dreams of making that chance a reality.

For 15 years, Bob continued to claim there was gold in the area. Unfortunately, Bob's drinking habits were too well known. He was a favorite of the low-rent sporting ladies in Colorado City, located just west of Colorado Springs. It was said he could lean down from his horse and pick up a whiskey bottle with his teeth. But because Bob was known to over-imbibe, and since most of Colorado's gold booms were coming to a close, the general public believed Womack's claims were nothing more than babble.

Working in the high country meadows, however, Bob Womack never could rid himself of the itch to find gold. Riding through the hills daily, Womack kept his eyes peeled for outcroppings and other clues to gold deposits. He found success in 1878 when he discovered a piece of "float," a piece of rock that breaks off when an outcropping erodes to the surface of the earth. These outcroppings contained types of rocks called porphyry and rhyolite. Today, Porphyry Street in Cripple Creek and Rhyolite Mountain north of town are tributes to these minerals.

Because of the volcanic formations in the Cripple Creek District, float is normally gray or even purple in color. It is hard to recognize as gold ore since the gold color is often not visible until the rock is processed or heated up. In addition, the gold found in the district is not placer gold like the type panned for in rivers and streams; rather, the gold is "hard rock," meaning it can only be dug or blasted out. It is no wonder that it took look so long to find the Cripple Creek bonanza.

Bob's float assayed at $200 per ton of gold ore. Certain he had found fortune at last, Womack boasted to anyone who would listen. Unfortunately, his stage was usually a barroom, his microphone a bottle of whiskey, and his audience a room full of hard drinkers who hardly took stock in a drunken cowboy's ramblings. For years, no one believed Bob's claim that there was gold in Cripple Creek and an 1884 hoax, in which the general public was duped by a fake claim, didn't help.

The hoax was the brainchild of three men. They were Captain H.B. Grose, who had a homestead in the district, plus two men from Leadville. In April of 1884, the con artists "salted" a hole with gold ore on some government land at

Bob Womack was in his 40s when his claims of gold in the district were finally substantiated. (Courtesy Ray Drake Collection, Cripple Creek District Museum.)

Divide went by a variety of names, including Bellevue after a nearby ranch, Theodore, and Rhyolite City. The most popular name appears to have been Hayden's Divide after Ferdinand V. Hayden's Geographical Survey team visited the area in the 1870s. (Courtesy Cripple Creek District Museum.)

Mount McIntyre, 13 miles west of Mt. Pisgah. Next, they staked the claim with a fake sign reading, "Teller Placer, Twenty Acres. S.J. Bradley, Locator: Discovered April 5, 1884. Surveyed by D.G. Miller, M.E., April 7, 1884."

The only thing left to do was alert the media. Accordingly, Captain Grose rode throughout the land telling everyone along the Florissant stage road and points beyond about the "gold discovery." The rush was on, with would-be miners leaving their homesteads from as far away as Fairplay and Leadville. In the meantime, Bradley and Miller had departed for Canon City, where their ore from Mount McIntyre magically assayed for $2,000 to the ton. Investors came out of the woodwork as Canon City anticipated reaping the benefits of such a find. And the Denver newspapers got so excited, they mistakenly called the new claim the Mt. Pisgah Discovery.

Just as all the merchants, miners, stage drivers, assayers, and railroads were prepared to rake in the massive fortunes, good old Bob Womack stepped in. As an expert on the terrain he had surveyed for years, Womack knew something was wrong with the picture. A quick ride out to Mt. McIntyre confirmed Bob's suspicion. Other experienced miners at the sight agreed the claim had been salted. Bradley and Miller escaped prosecution, but it was over a week before news of the fake claim got around.

Soon after the Mt. Pisgah Hoax, the caldera simmered down to quiet ranching life once more. But as more folks began exploring the Cripple Creek District as cattle country, Womack's story fell on new ears. He staked his first claim in 1886,

Winfield Scott Stratton gave a more youthful portrait when he joined the A&A Scottish Rite of Denver in 1896. Within a very short time, Stratton's wealth would turn him into an embittered millionaire with a melancholy fondness for alcohol. (Courtesy Cripple Creek District Museum.)

taking in partners who in turn staked other claims in the area. Ranchers in the area no doubt kept an open mind regarding Womack's claims. Over the last decade, the cattle industry around the district had suffered a series of blows. The introduction of barbed wire in 1873 created a number of land wars. By the 1880s, fencing had become a major issue and the Interior Department was called in to enforce illegal fence removal. Overgrazing began resulting in skimpier herds. Then, thousands of cattle were killed during an especially bad winter in 1886 and 1887. Ranchers were feeling the pinch and likely questioning their futures in the Pikes Peak region.

Just over Pikes Peak, residents outside of the district were recognizing the vacation qualities of Ute Pass, with more towns and attractions popping up regularly. At the top of the pass, the town of Bellevue, named after a nearby ranch and later known as Divide, was established in about 1886. An official carriage road was built to the top of Pikes Peak in 1888. As the population increased, so did Bob's chances of a viable partner to grubstake him by investing in his food and clothing in return for half of whatever Bob found. Money from an 1887 grubstake from Edwin Wallace was gone by 1889, but Bob managed to secure another partner in his dentist, Dr. John P. Grannis.

Nobody in Colorado Springs seemed interested in the find, which resembled dirty gray rock and looked of little value. Bob refused to give up. One night on one of his frequent visits to the city jail, Womack told two firemen his tale. The men were James Doyle and James Burns, whose subsequent investments in Cripple

Creek mines would go down in history and make both firemen millionaires. A few months later, Bob hit pay dirt and discovered the El Paso Lode. By 1891, Bob Womack's dream was finally realized. The Cripple Creek District saw an amazingly large and fast influx of people. They came from other mining camps around the state, as well as the east and other western mining towns.

By the time Womack's claims were substantiated, he was in his mid-40s. The boom of the Cripple Creek District—one of the last of its kind in America—was fast and furious. Within months, the district was crawling with prospectors. Hastily thrown up tents turned to camps and camps turned to towns. All evidence of Ute presence in the area was obliterated, save for one area known as Squaw Gulch where the remains of a Native American woman were found. For a short time, Papoose Gulch was also noted on local maps. Mines and mills sprang up almost daily as the district churned out over 28 millionaires in just a few years. Most of them were in their late 30s to mid-40s. One of them, the first millionaire in the district, was Womack's friend Winfield Scott Stratton.

Unlike Stratton, however, Bob was not meant to strike it rich. He owned at least three claims, if not more. Somehow, though, he never quite made money from his subsequent business deals. Some of his claims were sold for shamefully low prices and folklore is rampant with tales about him trading mines for bar tabs. For Bob Womack, being wealthy beyond his means was not a priority. On Christmas morning of 1893, for instance, Bob Womack celebrated the infamous sale of his Womack Placer by standing in front of Becker and Nolon's Saloon in Cripple Creek and passing out dollar bills to children. A line formed. To his dismay, Womack noticed grown men standing in line, some of whom were returning for more money. Bob threw an angry punch, which was reciprocated and sent him sprawling. It was Johnny Nolon who picked Bob up from the dirt and had him escorted home.

In 1896, Bob was said to be selling real estate, but soon retired to his sister Lida's boarding house in Colorado Springs. Bob's vision of a wealthy mining district, however, came to fruition throughout the rest of his life. They say Bob Womack died in poverty, but this isn't really the case. He lived out his life at Lida's, working around the property and living the same comfortable lifestyle he was used to. Following a last visit to Cripple Creek in 1904, Bob suffered a stroke. He passed away in 1909, forgotten by many. Today, his memory lives on as the man who discovered gold in the Cripple Creek District.

2. The Birth of a Gold Boom (1892–1893)

Between the years of 1891 and 1893, a number of camps, towns, and cities sprang up in the Cripple Creek District. Twenty-four square miles left a lot of ground to be covered and it wasn't long before the entire district was dotted with mines, tents, and camps. Miners, prospectors, and other would-be millionaires were arriving in droves via Ute Pass from the east or stage roads from the north, west, and south. It was only natural for some of the camps to evolve into permanent cities. By the end of the district's reign in the early 1900s, there would be approximately 25 such settlements in the region, with an additional 65 settlements located within a 40-mile radius.

Only a few communities existed in the immediate area prior to the gold rush of 1891. One was Bison, an 1860s logging camp located northeast of the district on the backside of Pikes Peak. In all probability, if Bison was still producing by 1891, it was quickly depleted by the rush. Another, more important community was known as Four Mile, located along what is now Teller County Road 1 from the town of Florissant to Cripple Creek. Teller One, as it is locally known, was originally part of a stage road that today is a smooth ride through high country prairie.

Roughly halfway between Florissant and Cripple Creek, a sign pointing to the Four Mile Cemetery can be spotted to the south. The beginnings of Four Mile are sketchy. Curiously, the community never aspired to be a city with so much as a business district. Rather, the hub of Four Mile was centered close to the junction of High Park Road and Highway 9. A crossroads led to Canon City and Cripple Creek. Later, a tiny town initially called Idaville, then Freshwater, and now known as Guffey, also served as a destination. Four stage lines serviced the area, which benefitted from the centralized location. Three other small farming communities—High Park, Bare Hills, and Gold Springs—were located just miles from the junction. High Park's post office opened in 1896 and the peak population was about 100.

One of the earliest references to the area dates to 1869, when Major James B. Thompson noted 200 Utes who had a winter hunting camp on Four Mile Creek. Water was ample in the Four Mile region and most of the homesteaders in the area were farmers. Potatoes and cabbage were the major staple. Later, ranchers like George Harker purchased spreads to raise cattle. The presence of whites in Native American country was bound to result in some skirmishes. Throughout the winter of 1874 and 1875, Ute leader Ouray camped near Florissant with 600 other Utes. During their stay, one of the men recognized the horse of J. Pleasant Marksbery as belonging to his friend. Two Ute men reclaimed the horse and returned it to the camp, not realizing the horse had been traded sometime back to a Mr. Nat Colby.

When Marksbery learned what had happened, he confronted Ouray's war chief, Shewano. In the ensuing scuffle, Marksbery wrestled away Shewano's gun, claiming he would keep it until his horse was returned. Next, Marksbery appeared at the Ute camp with his son, waving a piece of paper he claimed to be a special order from his commanding officer. Naturally, the Utes had no idea what the paper was or what it said. Marksbery's son led the horse away from the camp, which Denver's *Rocky Mountain News* described as being located near Mt. Pisgah. The Native Americans gave chase upon discovering the "theft" and a Ute named Tabweah shot Marksbery dead off his horse.

Marksbery's tragic end did little to prevent settlers from homesteading. Other pioneers in the Four Mile area included Reverend David P. Long, first owner of the "Petrified Forest" situated in today's Florissant Fossil Beds. Shortly after claiming his land, Long returned from an extended trip to discover his ranch had been sold out from under him. Undaunted, he homesteaded on some land, which today parallels Teller One, and platted the Four Mile Cemetery near his homestead. A Confederate Civil War veteran, Long named one of his daughters

Just a few months after its inception, Fremont was built up quickly. Many pioneers were still living in tents, but there was already a livery stable, hotels, saloons, stores, restaurants, and a budding business district in place. (Courtesy Cripple Creek District Museum.)

Children and teacher pose at one of the schools at Four Mile, c. 1893. Two schools at opposite ends of the expansive Four Mile District served children lucky enough to come for lessons. (Courtesy Hoyte Collection, Cripple Creek District Museum.)

Atlanta Georgia. Atlanta grew up, married, and later penned a family history of the Four Mile area. The Wilsons and the Warners were also settlers in the Four Mile area. The Warners built a sawmill and ranch on Cobb Creek. Cyrus Warner would eventually begin his own successful hauling business, transporting lettuce, potatoes, and cattle.

As the popularity of Four Mile grew, more ranchers prospered in the area. Frank Welty had a ranch and stage stop in the area. Portions of the ranch today serve as a llama ranch next to Evergreen Station. When the gold boom began at the Cripple Creek District, a few settlers from Four Mile profited from early prospects. At that time, the original road to Cripple Creek led to the junction of Spring Creek and Four Mile Creek and through Four Mile Canyon. The closest post offices were at High Park, Florissant, and Cripple Creek. The Four Mile District had two schools, known as West Four Mile, or Lower Four Mile, and Upper Four Mile.

Just beyond the realm of the Four Mile District lay the town of Florissant. A post office was established in November of 1872, although there were settlers there before that time. The population of Florissant in 1887 reached 50 souls. The chief industries included logging, ice production, farming, and ranching. One of Florissant's most prominent citizens was a widow named Adeline Hornbek, who settled in 1878. Born in 1833, Adeline came out west in 1861 with her first husband, Simon A. Harker. Following Simon's death after the great Denver flood of 1864, Adeline became prominent in financial affairs and managed to build up substantial wealth for a woman of her era. She remarried for a time to Elliot Hornbek, but the couple parted ways in about 1875. By the time she arrived in Florissant, Adeline had secured 160 acres of land that Simon Harker applied for prior to his death.

Bureau of Land Management records show Adeline's name on the original deed for her land, located 2 miles south of Florissant on Teller One. It is presumed Adeline lived in Florissant while building an impressive ranch house on her property. Adeline's wealth permitted her to build bigger and better than other homesteaders. Subsequently, her two-story home consisted of four bedrooms, a parlor, and a full kitchen including pantry. Water was hauled from nearby Grape Creek for cooking and washing. Other buildings were constructed as well: a milk house, chicken coop, large corral, stables, and a root cellar. The ranch was completed in about 1878, when it was valued at a whopping $1,200.

Adeline insulated her home with newspapers of 1879, many of which remain on the walls today. The papers served to keep dust from blowing between the chinked log walls and provided entertainment during the long winter evenings. In some areas, Adeline was even able to wallpaper her walls, a luxury few women in her circumstances enjoyed. Adeline's home especially was built with care, indicating that she hired skilled craftsmen to do the work. Two or three hands worked at the ranch, as well as Adeline's four teen-aged children. Besides raising cattle and horses, the family also grew potatoes, vegetables, and hay. By these means, Adeline was able to support herself while becoming a respected citizen in Florissant. In 1880, she served on the school board and was active enough in civic affairs to merit mention in both the *Crystal Peak Beacon* and the *Florissant Eagle*, both newspapers that published in Florissant.

The Four Mile Dance Hall and Community Center was renovated with state historic funds a few years ago. As one of the only known structures from Four Mile to remain standing, the hall still hosts occasional entertainment with dances featuring local bands.

At the ripe age of 61 years in 1899, Adeline remarried again to 46-year-old Frederick B. Sticksel, a German immigrant from Denver who may have been in her employ. The younger husband caused much consternation among Adeline's family and friends. Sticksel was also a divorcee, whose last marriage had ended just over a year before in Colorado Springs. So disgruntled was Adeline's family by this revelation that they declined to buy her a headstone when she died in 1905. A tombstone has since been purchased to mark Adeline's grave and her ranch is a living history museum.

Another community prior to the formation of the Cripple Creek District was Touraine. Little is known about Touraine except that its post office began on November 9, 1889. It was most likely a ranching community located near the later town of Cameron. Ranching had already taken an upswing when the boom at Cripple Creek began. The rush gave ranchers and farmers alike an opportunity to market their goods at Cripple Creek, rather than Canon City or Colorado Springs and points far beyond. During the 1890s, ranch hands were paid $2.50 a day to plant and harvest, with profits in Cripple Creek yielding roughly $10 a load. Farm-grown goods were a welcome relief to the first arrivals in the Cripple Creek District, most of whom brought only what supplies they could purchase in Colorado City and lug up Ute Pass.

Ranchers bringing their fresh vegetables to sell in Cripple Creek were no doubt amazed at what they saw upon their arrival. What had been quiet country similar to their own expansive homesteads suddenly resembled a war zone. Trees were being cut down and hewn into lumber. Streets were materializing along the hillsides below Mt. Pisgah, and new buildings were springing up like wildfire. And it was all under the supervision of two men named Horace Bennett and Julius Myers, whose presence had already been known for some time.

It was a drop in the hat for Horace Bennett to buy Cripple Creek. Having come west from Michigan in 1883, Bennett first settled himself in Denver. A greenhorn at 21 years of age, he couldn't do better than selling furniture at first. But Horace Bennett wasn't the average salesman. By 1884, he was setting up a real estate office on Seventeenth Street in Denver. Within a year, Bennett took Julius A. Myers on as a partner and formed the firm of Bennett & Myers. Myers was 37 years old in 1885, 15 years older than Bennett and no doubt more experienced in real estate. It was probably he who wisely decided to test the realty waters all over the state.

In July, Bennett and Myers made a trip to what was soon to be known as the Cripple Creek District. They purchased the Pikes Peak Land and Cattle Company, consisting of four homesteads, including one that had belonged to rancher William Womack. The seller was Phillip Ellsworth, who had himself paid $75,000 for the land before realizing it was good for nothing more than cattle grazing. Ellsworth was only too glad to unload what he considered a white elephant.

The land Bennett and Myers purchased amounted to about 640 acres. The selling price was $5,000 down, with $20,000 remaining. Following the transaction, Horace renamed the expanded ranch the Houseman Cattle and Land Company after Alexander Houseman, the man hired to oversee the

Today, the Hornbek Homestead is a living history museum. Adeline's home remains in its original location with several area buildings added to recreate the ranch as it was during her lifetime. During the summer months, the museum is open daily with special events.

property. Next, Bennett hired George Carr out of Kansas to come manage the old Welty homestead. Bennett hardly cared that Carr chose to call the place the Broken Box Ranch. He and Myers had other investments to deal with in Denver. The two returned to Denver and waited for something good to happen with their land at Cripple Creek.

They didn't have to wait long. In October of 1890, Womack and Grannis finally hit pay dirt with the El Paso Lode, whose ore assayed for $250 in gold to the ton. By February of 1891, prospectors were flocking to the district. Florissant also flourished as the newspapers claimed gold had been found at the nearby Hensley Ranch. For a brief time, the tiny railroad town was flooded with miners and their claims. Within a few weeks, the claims were found to be untrue and the mining gypsies moved on to the Cripple Creek District, adding to the massive influx of people.

Bennett and Myers knew just what to do. First, they conferred with Alexander Houseman and George Carr. The Colorado gold rush had been going on since 1859 and all four veterans of gold booms past knew that mining was a constant gamble. Already, Colorado had seen hundreds of boom camps come and go. The

27

chance of hitting another gold boom after so many years of dormancy was small and the men had little faith in this newest strike. Rather than investing in the mines, the men opted instead to strike it rich by platting a town. Bennett named it Fremont after explorer John C. Fremont.

According to postal records, a post office was established at Fremont in July of 1891. A little over three months later, on November 6, 80 acres were platted. No sooner had the name been filed when people began flooding into town as fast as lots could sell. The Colorado Midland Railroad increased its runs to three trains a day, stopping at Florissant to unload passengers and supplies bound for Cripple Creek. Tents, cabins, and shacks sprang up everywhere. Consequently, the town of Cripple Creek was laid out so haphazardly that Fremont resembled a miniature San Francisco with all of its funny hills and curves. Even today, one of two original terraces in Cripple Creek illustrates how Bennett Avenue actually spans the length of a hillside.

Sure of the district's failure, Bennett and Myers made sure each lot deed came with the stipulation that all lumber was to be left behind when the property was abandoned. In accordance with the social graces of the day, the Fremont plat

Horace Bennett and Julius Myers made a winning pair, in spite of an age difference of 15 years. Little did the two men know when they platted the city of Cripple Creek that Bennett Avenue would become the most important thoroughfare in town, while Myers Avenue was destined to be the heart of the red light district. (Courtesy Cripple Creek District Museum.)

also allowed liquor and gambling. Bennett and Myers named the two principle streets after themselves, with the streets of Warren, Carr, and Eaton completing the city's hub. By Thanksgiving of 1891, Fremont consisted of 30 platted blocks containing 766 lots. Each lot measured 25 feet wide and 125 feet deep. The lots sold at $25 each or $50 for corner lots. Within a year, those same lots would sell for $250 or more.

The rapid property sales enticed some investors from Colorado Springs to plat 140 acres near Fremont and get in on the lot sales. The group called their plat Hayden Placer and offered lots and buildings on a payment plan. They also restricted gambling and liquor sales, giving Bennett & Myers a competitive edge. But both towns were becoming a real estate whirlwind. In just two months, they had a combined population of 600 to 800 people. Still, the battle between the two raged on. For unknown reasons, Fremont lost its post office on December 9. Then, on February 4, 1892, Hayden Placer filed a post office name of Morland.

When postal authorities accepted Morland, Bennett & Myers filed a plat on the northeastern most section of the former Broken Box Ranch, near the settlement of Touraine, and called it Cripple Creek. In addition, the real estate kings platted another part of the homestead and called it Arequa. Next, they took out a classy advertisement in Denver, extolling the virtues of Fremont. "Fremont is the only incorporated city in this District," read the ad in part. "Fremont has a population of 4000. Fremont will be lighted by electricity by April 15th. Fremont is the terminal point for all stages from Canon City and Florissant." Over 1,000 lots had been sold to date, the ad boasted, and a $10,000 hotel was slated to open by May 1.

By then, however, the Cripple Creek Gold Mining District name had caught on. In June, the name of the post office was changed back to Fremont, but finally the name Cripple Creek won out on June 20. The post office assigned the Cripple Creek name to both Fremont and Hayden Placer. Bennett and Myers returned victorious, to their lofty Denver office. From there, they oversaw the Fremont Electric Light and Power Company Plant premier in 1892 and worked with coroner Oscar Lampman to establish Mt. Pisgah Cemetery in 1893. The first telephone in the district also made its debut. Things at Cripple Creek ran smoothly, with only one exception: as Cripple Creek quickly grew, the city's prostitutes were unceremoniously banned from plying their trade on Bennett Avenue. Accordingly, the ladies moved their trunks and coverlets one block south to Myers Avenue.

It is said that Julius Myers was a religious man and a red-light district flourishing on his namesake street was no doubt difficult to fathom in his mind. Both Myers and Bennett, however, were too concerned with their other investments to worry too much about it. The two remained in Denver and early directories give no indication of a residence for either man. The Bennett & Myers office at Carr and Eaton Avenues simply retained a resident agent. They say Bennett and Myers never even owned a mine in the district. They didn't need to. Aside from their other investments, they made a quick and painless $1 million off the lots at Fremont, plus lot sales at the nearby town of Arequa.

Beyond Myers Avenue, Poverty Gulch was comprised of the lowest prostitutes, drug addicts, alcoholics, criminals, and the poorest families. (Courtesy Cripple Creek District Museum.)

Arequa was located in the gulch nearest the Mt. Pisgah Mining District. The lot sales there proved to be quite successful, selling for a total profit of $320,000. Streets in Arequa were gallantly named after past presidents of the United States. The town's name, however, actually stemmed back to 1873 when a man known as "Uncle" Benjamin Requa had a general store and eatery at Fountain, south of Colorado Springs. It was in this store that Bob Womack met up with Ferdinand V. Hayden, whose men later surveyed the Cripple Creek District for the U.S. Geological and Geographical Survey of the Territories. In Ben Requa's honor, Bob Womack called the surveyed gulch Arequa. No one is sure how that "A" got in there.

Later, Bennett and Myers kept the name when they platted the town. A post office was established in July of 1894, but was discontinued a mere two months later. Postal records note "establishment rescinded," but give no reason. There was also a cemetery at Arequa, but the graves were moved to a cemetery at the nearby city of Victor decades ago. Unfortunately, the terrain was too rough for building and the area too far from the mines. Despite its promising status, Arequa never topped more than 100 residents. Arequa's biggest claim to fame was the Arequa Mill, a chlorination plant built at a cost of $532,000. For a time, the plant was successful. In time, however, Arequa became absorbed by the communities of Eclipse, Elkton, and Beacon. In 1900, the total population of these four towns was 2,500.

A third town was established in February of 1892 as well. At the far southern end of the Cripple Creek District, the homestead of Victor C. Adams was sectioned off to include the town of Lawrence. The post office was established at the same time. Just a month later, another tiny community called Barry sprang up between Cripple Creek and Lawrence. One Horace Barry had made his way into Squaw Gulch and struck it mildly rich. Barry founded a town in his own name and prophesied the hamlet would become the "cultural center" of the district. Although Barry merely consisted of a few log cabins and some tents, its founding father set off a wave of optimism that seemed to affect everyone who came there.

In the meantime, the Colorado Midland Railroad was making plans to expand to the district. The railroad had already made its way up Ute Pass to the tiny hamlet of what was first called Bellevue, then platted as Rhyolite City, known once as Theodore, renamed Hayden's Divide, and later shortened to just plain Divide. The tiny town did more than service travelers along Ute Pass. Divide was also prominent in farming and was especially known for its lettuce, which was shipped on to both Cripple Creek, Colorado Springs, and other points. In its time, Divide was dubbed the "Lettuce Capital of the World."

At Divide, Hayden's Toll Road turned towards Cripple Creek, 18 miles away. As the gold rush pressed on, the Colorado Midland began building its Midland Terminal spur along this road in an effort to reach Cripple Creek. Roughly 10 miles outside of Divide, the community of Midland was constructed in June of 1892 to service first the construction workers and later the railroad itself. Midland's first buildings were a Midland Terminal Depot and the spacious Midland Hotel. The new railroad was a sign of good things to come.

In 1893, Congress repealed the Sherman Silver Purchase Act, making silver virtually worthless. Just three years before, the United States government had

Lawrence was the first camp to be located in what is now Victor. This is one of the only known photographs of the town. (Courtesy Mazzulla Collection, Cripple Creek District Museum.)

Barry's population consisted of citizens from all walks of life. Families' homes were intermingled with those of prostitutes and gamblers. For the most part, however, Barry constituted a quiet working-class town with neat rows of middle- to lower-class homes. (Courtesy Cripple Creek District Museum.)

passed the act and started buying silver during a nationwide recession. It was a feeble plan that did little to alleviate the recession. The government repealed the Sherman Silver Act and stopped buying silver. During the ensuing panic, thousands of silver millionaires, miners, and whole towns literally lost their money, not to mention their way of life. For many miners, the gold of the Cripple Creek District offered a viable way out of their newfound unemployment. More miners than ever traipsed over the mountains towards the district, the glint of gold in their hungry eyes.

By then, the little town of Barry was in full swing. Its gold mills were running full blast, with the Blue Bell Mine employing most of the population. There were shops and eating houses, as well as two or three neat rows of homes. Almost all of the structures were constructed of wood, with dirt streets and nary a sidewalk in sight. The Squaw Gulch Amusement Club, along with a handful of prostitutes, kept miners entertained.

Just up the road from Barry, another hamlet sprouted called Mound City. The new camp's post office opened in March of 1893. In just over a year, however, both Mound City and Barry had lost their population to the much larger town of Anaconda just up the gulch. Other camps and towns that became suburbs of or were absorbed by Anaconda included Jackpot near the Jackpot Mine and Glory Hole, the place name for an area at the top of Squaw Gulch between Anaconda and Midway. By today's landmarks, Anaconda's main drag was to the right of Highway 67 heading toward Victor. On the other side of the road, another street ran over a trestle and above the huge cribbing of the Mary McKinney Mine. In

1893, Anaconda had three saloons: Good's Place, Mayer & Cook, and Page & Allen. The Anaconda Dance Hall provided entertainment for miners. With its vices set firmly in place, Anaconda became incorporated in 1894.

The next town to appear in 1893 grew to be the second largest in the Cripple Creek District. This was Victor, located at the base of Battle Mountain very near most of the mines that were making the district famous. Victor was named for the same Victor C. Adams who had established Lawrence in 1892. By 1893, Victor was already populated with shacks and tents. Mines literally surrounded the camp on nearly every side, with more claims being staked every day.

As the city took shape, Frank and Harry Woods, along with their father, Warren, came to the area. The threesome hailed from Illinois, where Harry had dabbled in the newspaper business. Back in 1878, Harry had already tried his luck at the silver camp of Leadville. Frank and Warren soon joined him and when their venture failed, the three returned to the east. The family came to Colorado again in 1892 to try their luck once more when news of the Cripple Creek gold rush hit. Having dabbled in real estate before, the men arrived in Victor and incorporated the Woods Investment Company in June of 1893 to promote Victor. A post office was established in June of 1894 at an elevation of 9,729 feet and Victor was dubbed the "City of Mines."

Last but certainly not least came the high altitude town of Altman, which had its beginnings in September of 1893. The town was named for Mr. Samuel Altman,

Colorado photographer William H. Jackson took several photographs around the Cripple Creek District, including this view of Anaconda. (Courtesy Jackson Collection, Cripple Creek District Museum.)

who ran a sawmill in Cripple Creek and built the first stamp mill there. Later, he purchased the Free Coinage Mine on Bull Hill before founding his namesake town. Situated at 10,700 feet on Bull Hill near Bull Cliff, Altman soon held the record as the highest incorporated city in the continental United States. From the lofty township, Victor could be seen below. To the northeast, Pikes Peak provided a stunning backdrop for the town.

If Altman was looking to progress into a modern town, however, Mayor Thomas Ferroll had his own ideas. When the Colorado Telephone Company attempted to install telephone poles in town, Ferroll retaliated by chopping two of the poles down. Ferroll was made to pay for the poles, as well as the wages of the telephone workers who reinstalled the lines. Altman ultimately succeeded in obtaining a single telephone, located at Morrison and McMillan's store. The town's success was guaranteed. Surrounded by over 100 producing mines, Altman saw a steady flow of miners and merchants moving to town. The population was said to have soared to over 2,000 by 1894. In time, Altman would also serve another purpose as the Cripple Creek District surged into the first of two bloody and violent labor wars.

At an altitude of 10,700 feet, Altman was at one time said to be the highest incorporated town in the world. Despite its lofty location, Altman provided every modern convenience and played an integral role in the labor wars of both 1893–1894 and 1903–1904. (Courtesy Cripple Creek District Museum.)

3. THE FIRST OF TWO LABOR STRIKES (1893–1894)

Historically, interpretation of the word "fairness" has affected every civilization. Sooner or later, human nature dictates the feeling of being treated unfairly in some respect. Apply this aspect of human nature to work ethics and the result is dissension among both employers and employees. Such was the case in the infamous labor strikes of the Cripple Creek District. The district's first labor strike began in 1893, with much violence and mayhem. Mines were blown up during the foray, and shoot-outs resulted in injuries and death. Eventually, the militia was brought in. By then, the strike was receiving nationwide media coverage.

It all started when various mine workers began comparing notes on who made what. It was soon apparent that some miners were making $3 for an eight-hour day of work, while others worked an extra hour or more to earn their three bills. The pay was normal for the day, but most miners were a poor lot who struggled to survive daily. The average miner paid between $1.75 per week for an unfurnished house and $2.50 per week in a boarding house that included furnishings, baths, and meals.

Many miners first arrived in the district without their families, who had remained in the east or at some other mining town until the prospects looked good. Often, the families were extended to include uncles, cousins, brothers, sons, fathers, and even grandparents. Occasionally, an entire clan or nationality would form its own community. Such was the case with the McCormacks, whose family settled near Lawrence in 1891 and soon formed a colony numbering over 100 Scotsmen.

Upon arriving in the Cripple Creek District, the McCormacks changed the spelling of their name to McCormick in order to pass themselves off as Irishmen. Even in those early days, the district quickly established class among its communities. Because the Cripple Creek District's gold boom was among the last in the state, most of the arriving miners were veterans in the industry or descended from those who were. In a place where the gold rush promised to be the biggest one in Colorado, towns such as Cripple Creek hurried to establish

The Labor War of 1893 and 1894 made headlines across the country. Americans were by now used to reading about labor wars throughout the state. Miners everywhere voiced their displeasure at working too hard for too little money. (Courtesy Cripple Creek District Museum.)

a caste system among nationalities after the fashion of an upper-class, white-collar city.

Over one-third of the district's citizens were white, Irish, and Catholic. Italians, Japanese, Greeks, Mexicans, Hungarians, Austrians, Slavs, and even Finns were among those banned outright from mining, let alone living, in the district. The other two-thirds of the populace were comprised of direct descendants of immigrants or newly arrived foreigners. Cornishmen and Irishmen made some of the finest miners in the state, descending from generations of miners in their homelands. The Cornish in particular had mining roots going back to the 1850s and beyond.

Swedes formed another ethnic group, growing enough in number to merit publishing their own newspaper, *Svenska Posten*. Hundreds of French people were also present, many of them maintaining commercial businesses. Chinese and African Americans were tolerated, but they were fewer in number than in other mining districts, usually securing employment by running laundry rooms or working as porters in the saloons. Chinese were highly discouraged from working in the mines and only a handful of African-American miners are on record today.

Notably, few of the prostitutes working around the district were Irish, but there was a good mix of German, Black, Chinese, and French girls in the industry.

Even the "white" mining families lived a lower-middle-class existence. There were usually more mouths to feed than money to feed them. The wife of a miner could expect to spend her days making meals, cutting wood, keeping a fire stoked, cleaning, sewing, washing, shopping, and taking care of the household in general. Families living closest to the mines endured daily blasting, which sent dirt and dust flying over everything. Illness among children and adults was common, especially with a blatant lack of medical facilities in the district in 1893; therefore, miner's wives also frequently served as nursemaids, midwives, and funeral directors. It was not unusual for a family of eight to start out living in a one- or two-room house. Miners who stayed at their jobs and received promotions could later move the family into more expansive quarters.

At $3 a day, it is no wonder expenses were tight. Both married and single miners were also known to frequent the saloons and gambling houses after work. Miners in general were hardworking, hard-drinking men. In 1893, there were over 13 sample rooms (an early fancy name for a tavern) and dance halls in Cripple Creek. Anaconda had four saloons to its name and there were six bars at Altman. In 1894, the nearby city of Victor sported five bars. Several "lunch rooms" offered such deals as a sandwich and beer for just a nickel or a dime. Similar incentives awaited miners in the gambling halls and the blue-collar brothels, whose girls charged an average of 50¢ to $1, plus all the drinks and tips they could finagle. All served as

Mattie Stockton Banta's wedding party at Barry, c. 1893. Women relished attending social outings; weddings especially gave them a chance to dress up and escape from dreary housechores. (Courtesy Banta Collection, Cripple Creek District Museum.)

a temptation and many a divorce was granted on "grounds of non-support." The man who made it home with all of his pay in hand was a strong and determined man indeed.

Life was perhaps somewhat easier for the single miner, who could rent a room in a boardinghouse, stay at a hotel, or room with several men in one house. At the camps nearest the mines, miners could expect to share a tent with others. Unless their meals were part of the rent, most single men ate out daily and spent their time off wandering the saloons. Housing shortages were common. Some saloon owners, such as Johnny Nolon of Cripple Creek, offered up their pool tables at closing so men could have a place to sleep. Miners taking up such offers as this would awaken in a drunken haze, arriving at work with little sleep, dirty clothes, no bath, and an empty stomach.

The average workday for a miner in 1893 was grueling compared to today's standards. Safety standards were minimal and primitive. A hoist bucket bringing miners up from deep inside the shaft could break, sending the men plummeting hundreds of feet or killing the miners below. Injuries and death by dangerous fumes, cave ins, or falling rocks were common. When blasting, the miners would feed live sticks of dynamite into a series of holes drilled in rock. The men were supposed to count as each blast went off. A miscalculation or missed shot could have agonizingly fatal results.

Losing body parts, having one's head blown off, and other horribly gruesome accidents were common. In later years, one physician would recall how one mining accident victim was thought to be dead. The poor man had been caught

Miners were hard-working, industrious men laboring for low pay at high risk. Fatal accidents and job-related illnesses were common in the industry. A typical miner's widow was lucky to receive compensation from the mine and often received handouts from sympathetic fellow miners and their families instead. (Courtesy Cripple Creek District Museum.)

Thousands of prospectors and miners from all over the world flocked into the district during its heyday. Although his nationality is unknown, judging by his hat and outfit, miner J.A. Jensen was probably new to America. (Courtesy Cripple Creek District Museum.)

in an explosion and arrived at the mortuary with most of the lower half of his face missing, his arms blown off at the elbow, and one leg slung clear up over his shoulder. Some hours later, the physician was horrified to discover the "corpse" was still alive and found him actually sitting up and moving around. "I was of no service except to give hypodermic injection or two to the mangled object in the coffin," the physician remembered. "It lived until nearly morning."

Widows and families of such victims rarely received more than a small stipend from the mine, plus the sympathy of their neighbors. Miners who met their end while at work were quickly replaced and death was immediately forgotten by the mine owners. If the mines were unsympathetic to injuries and deaths of their miners, they were even more so to their live employees. Breaks were unheard of and lunch time was minimal, with men often eating as they worked for their $3 per day. Add lack of benefits, no vacation, and humiliating daily strip searches to keep the gold with the mine where it belonged, and unrest over a nine-hour workday was inevitable.

When the Isabella Mining Company and its three mines tried to extend the work day, employees lost no time in instituting the first strike by walking out on the job (some sources claim the first mine to impose the nine-hour day was the Buena Vista Mine, not the Isabella). The Isabella immediately rescinded its new policy, but five more mines announced a nine-hour schedule on January 17, 1894.

Enter Free Coinage Union No. 19 of the Western Federation of Miners (WFM), which a Scottish miner named John Calderwood organized in January of 1893. Calderwood, allegedly a West Point graduate, succeeded in forming unions at Victor, Anaconda, and Cripple Creek. Before long, 800 miners had joined the WFM. This determined bunch maintained that a legal workday should consist of no more than eight hours. In reply, many mine owners insisted that their longer shifts remain in place.

More mines joined suit and the nine-hour day was upheld by 12 district mines as of February 1. Ironically, one of them was owned by none other than Sam Altman, founder of the town that now represented union miners. Within hours of the decree, nearly 500 nine-hour workers left their jobs. About one-third of the mines in the district were affected. The mine owners did nothing at first, anticipating that the strikers would run out of money and come back to work. By March, however, many miners had secured jobs in eight-hour mines and appeared to be doing just fine.

In quiet and proud desperation, the mine owners next offered to settle for an eight-hour shift, but demanded a 50¢ cut in the daily pay. The WFM adamantly denied the offer. At the time, union workers, including those miners working in eight-hour mines, were being assessed 10 percent of their earnings for union dues. This no doubt led to some resentment among striking and non-striking miners. Longtime friends parted ways and families were divided.

Soon, the district was segregated into union and non-union businesses, both of whom were contributing to the cause. In Cripple Creek, the Colorado Trading and Transfer Company's A.E. Carlton allegedly had little tolerance or sympathy for the striking miners. Years before, Carlton and William K. Gillett had purchased a former warehouse from John H. Eisenhart and converted it to a freight and storage company. The new Colorado Trading and Transfer Company later went into business with the Midland Terminal Railroad in Cripple Creek and, within three years, Carlton was among the richest men in town. Later, he owned and operated the First National Bank of Cripple Creek. The strikes were damaging his business, not to mention causing unrest. One day, before shipping out a load of wheat that he knew was going to some pro-union boys, Carlton was said to have hopped up on the freight wagon and urinated on the load before sending it on its way.

The trickle effect filtered all the way down to the schools, where even children began choosing their playmates more carefully and fighting among themselves. Others, such as E.W. Giddings, took full advantage of the strike by offering produce at exorbitant prices. Giddings shipped an entire train carload of apples from Colorado Springs to Cripple Creek and managed to sell every single one at $1 apiece.

In the meantime, mine owners succeeded in procuring court orders to cease striking, but they were to no avail. The town of Altman had already been declared a union town. As the highest town in the district, Altman afforded views in all directions and offered relative security from invading forces. The WFM quickly secured itself there among 1,200 residents. Ultimately, they succeeded in closing the town to all but union men and membership cards were required of anyone wishing to enter town.

Altman's defensive tactics angered the mine owners, whose mines were suffering noticeably from a lack of employees. The war escalated into heated intensity as the mine owners hired a number of temporary deputies to disperse the miners at Altman. During one encounter, sheriff's deputies on their way to Altman were accosted by the town's own police staff and disarmed. One deputy was wounded and two others were arrested for carrying concealed weapons.

The indecent acts at Altman enraged El Paso County Sheriff Frank Bowers, who demanded that Colorado Governor Davis H. Waite send in the Colorado State Militia. Unsure of the seriousness of the problem, but going by the sheriff's description of mayhem at the scene, Governor Waite allowed for 50 special sheriffs to be deputized at Colorado Springs. When officials at Altman protested, Governor Waite claimed Sheriff Bowers had told him a deputy was killed, not wounded.

In addition, Adjutant General Thomas J. Tarsney was hardly impressed when he arrived on the scene. Based on the mine owners' description, General Tarsney was expecting a maddened, riotous crowd. What he found instead was a bunch of disheartened but dedicated miners. By the time Bowers had secured 18 warrants for strikers on Bull Hill near Altman, Tarsney was ready to withdraw his offer of assistance. The accused men surrendered without incident. One was tried and acquitted, with the other 17 men being released without trial.

The state militia stands ready for action on Bull Hill. Riots, shootings, and looting were common during the labor war, resulting in a dangerous situation for miners and their families. (Courtesy Cripple Creek District Museum.)

Winfield Stratton's Independence Mine was located outside of Victor. Stratton's home is in the lower left corner and was likely the nicest home he ever occupied up to that time. Later, Stratton lived part-time at his own company town, Strattonville, before moving to more discreet quarters in Colorado Springs. (Courtesy Cripple Creek District Museum.)

At this point, Winfield Scott Stratton stepped forward. A former carpenter by trade, Stratton had started dabbling in mining as early as 1874. Urged by his friend Bob Womack, 42-year-old Stratton arrived in Cripple Creek in May of 1891 divorced, broke, and tired. With little faith in this latest boom, Stratton chose a spot to prospect that he calculated sat on the edge of the great caldera comprising the Cripple Creek District. Stratton's calculations paid off. His Independence Mine, staked on July 4, 1891, was yielding a whopping $50,000 to $100,000 per month by 1896.

By the time of the strikes, the Independence ranked as the third largest mine in the district. Other subsequent investments had made Stratton a millionaire almost overnight. Now wealthy far beyond his needs, he continued to live a somewhat simple life, preferring to donate his wealth rather than flaunt it. "Too much money is not good for any man," he once said. "I have too much and it is not good for me."

Still, having been in the position of a starving miner, Stratton sympathized with the men who worked for him. Already, his benevolent acts towards his employees had become legend to the toiling miners of the district. He was known to give raises at random. When one of his employees died on the job, he gave $3,000 to the miner's widow. He also once purchased a farm and presented it as a gift to a friend. In March, Stratton suggested a compromise: miners could work a nine-hour day for $3.25, or an eight-hour day for $3. The WFM accepted the offer, with Stratton signing a contract to put the deal into effect at his mines.

If Stratton was hoping his actions would be incentive to other mine owners, he was wrong. Most of the other mine owners balked and the situation was at a standstill once more. Things went from bad to worse. County officers began arresting striking miners and setting the bail too high for the union to pay. Mining company guards were becoming aggressive; there were some skirmishes. Within a short time, the mine owners retaliated further with a private army numbering between 900 and 1,200 deputies, plus 300 cavalrymen.

Altman's army only numbered 700, but the strikers knew what to do next. On May 25, they descended on the Strong Mine just outside of Victor, disarmed its guards, and blew up the mine just as a train full of anti-union men arrived. Amazingly, two train cars filled with former police and firefighters from Denver were unharmed. A mine superintendent and two other miners were in the Strong Mine at the time of the explosion, but also escaped with no more than a very bad case of shock. Next, the miners met a group of deputies from Colorado Springs. The two groups advanced on each other near Victor. When the smoke cleared, the deputies had retreated, leaving two miners dead. Five more striking miners were in their custody.

John Calderwood, who had left the district to recruit more union men, returned to a chaotic sight. Although he managed to settle everyone down upon returning to the scene, more unrest was sure to come. This time, Governor Waite was even more reluctant to step in than before. What had started over $3 per

The Strong Mine was in shambles after being blown up during the strikes. Ironically, photographer J.A. Harlan was conveniently on hand to photograph the scene both before and after the explosion. (Courtesy Cripple Creek District Museum.)

day had turned into a personal war of egos. The governor ordered the strikers to retreat, claiming they were assembling in unlawful bodies. While he was at it, the governor also ordered the deputy sheriffs to disperse. Neither would give in, although they did exchange the three men from the Strong Mine for the five strikers captured at the scene of the explosion. Ultimately, the governor himself made a trip to Altman to survey the carnage, then traveled back to Colorado Springs to mediate between the miners and their employers on the neutral grounds of Colorado College.

Once more, the governor suggested paying the miners their $3 for an eight-hour day. He also suggested that the striking miners be pardoned from any criminal acts they might have committed. After some discussion, the mine owners finally agreed to the wage deal, but refused to pardon the miners. By then, there were over 1,000 temporary deputies at Divide, just 18 miles from the district. None of them were listening to Sheriff Bowers, electing a county commissioner to lead them instead. Things were looking dangerous and at Bowers's request, Governor Waite called in the militia once more.

The remains of Philip Schuch's business in Cripple Creek are seen during the 1893 labor war. Under the guise of a "victory parade," angry anti-union deputies trashed and terrorized the city. (Courtesy Cripple Creek District Museum.)

As news of the strike spread around the country, more and more men on both sides gathered to fight for the cause. As many as 100 men hijacked a train and had traveled 100 miles from the Colorado mining town of Rico before being ordered back to their homes. Another 200 men were marching from Leadville. By some miracle, Governor Waite succeeded in calming them down. "Nothing can be gained by you by a battle," he told them, "but much can be won if you wait."

The miners waited. On June 4, a compromise was finally reached. The mine owners agreed once more to pay the $3 for an eight-hour shift. In turn, the strikers agreed to face the charges against them. By the time a settlement was secured, however, everyone was too riled up. Sheriff Bowers's uncontrollable army of 1,200 men continued their advance on Altman to seek revenge on the miners. Over the course of four days, the governor ordered them to disperse while Bowers attempted to get them back in control. Finally, on June 8, the governor ordered the state's troops, along with the National Guard, to intervene between the army and the miners' encampment. General Brooks of the state militia informed Bowers's army that the militia would open fire within 15 minutes if the troops did not turn back. That did the trick and the deputies backed off. After 130 days, the strike was finally over.

Sheriff Bowers, already embarrassed at the loss of control over his army, lost no time in complaining to Governor Waite. General Brooks's actions had interfered with law enforcement, he claimed. Furthermore, the sheriff demanded that the militia be put under his command. The governor no doubt laughed at such a silly request, especially coming from a subordinate sheriff in a mining camp. To add insult to injury, the governor ordered Adjutant General Tarsney to permit surrender of the miners without disarming them. As an additional safeguard, the governor furthermore ordered the state troops to protect the miners as they surrendered. This they did, with the miners willfully surrendering without incident. Many of them voluntarily turned over their firearms as well.

Bowers's troops were not only insulted by the miners' peaceful surrender, they were also angry that no skirmish had taken place. It seemed they were determined to have their fight, whether or not the war was over. When the deputies were warned a final time that any hostile moves would be countered with an attack by the militia, it was the last straw. The deputies ultimately took their anger out on the city of Cripple Creek. In the course of a "victory parade" down Bennett Avenue, 1,200 angry deputies rioted and looted stores while terrorized citizens ran for cover or cowered in their homes. The incident lasted several hours and it was night before order was restored.

As for Sheriff Bowers, he got some just reward by arresting strikers who had broken the law during the labor war. The deputies were gone, but the militia stayed on hand with the intent of protecting both miners and mine owners, as well as those under arrest. Of approximately 300 strikers who agreed to stand trial, one miner was convicted of robbery, but was later released by the State Supreme Court. Two other men were convicted of blowing up the Strong Mine. The men spent a short time in the State Penitentiary at Canon City, but were also later released. John Calderwood was acquitted.

Aside from the two men killed at Victor, Adjutant General Tarsney perhaps got the worst of it out of the labor strikes. Following the strike, General Tarsney traveled to Colorado Springs to testify in defense of the strikers on trial. On the night of June 22, Tarsney was kidnapped by a group of men led by ex-deputy Joe Wilson. Tarsney was summoned to the lobby of the Alamo Hotel under the premise of a phone call, nabbed, and taken to the edge of Colorado Springs where he was beaten, tarred, and feathered. From there, he was ordered to walk to Denver. Tarsney spent most of the night wandering along the Santa Fe Railroad tracks before finding aid at a ranch 10 miles north. Governor Waite sent a special train and Tarsney was returned to his Denver home.

Most of Tarsney's attackers also returned to their respective homes. Of the 15 men who took part in the escapade, 11 were eventually tracked down and arrested in Colorado Springs. One of the men who had helped kidnap Tarsney was Sherman Crumley, a hack driver who eventually moved to Victor and formed his own gang of thieves. In Tarsney's case, Crumley and his cohorts were released by Sheriff Bowers. As for the general, he did return to Colorado Springs—but not to testify on behalf of the striking miners. His kidnappers had made their wishes known. His refusal to testify resulted in a $50 fine, which no doubt added insult to injury. Afterwards, Tarsney returned to Denver, never to darken the portals of Cripple Creek mines again.

The town of Altman became a virtual fort during the 1893 and 1894 Labor War. Miners wishing to enter town were required to show a membership card to armed guards; the town was "closed" to all others, especially anyone sympathetic to the mine owners. (Courtesy Cripple Creek District Museum.)

4. THE COMING OF THE RAILROADS (1894–1896)

The labor wars of 1894 left both miners and their employers spent. In an amazingly short time, however, the Cripple Creek District was back to normal. There was no time to look at the past; the future was paved with gold. More and more towns were forming and the Midland Terminal Railroad was being built over the former toll road from Divide to Cripple Creek.

Prior to the Midland, Cripple Creek had relied solely on stage roads for transportation in and out of the district. The earliest of these was the Cheyenne Toll Road, which wound up Cheyenne Canyon from Colorado Springs to join today's Gold Camp Road. The route had originally been established in 1875 as the Cheyenne & Beaver Toll Road. The road saw continued use over time, gaining popularity in 1891 as a shorter, 30-mile route from Colorado Springs to Lawrence. Promoters of the road spent $18,000 to improve it and the Cheyenne Toll Road proved very useful until about 1895.

From the south, a second route into the Cripple Creek District was via Shelf Road, a precarious and dangerous trail that wound around steep canyon walls with cliff-hanging drop offs. Ten miles outside of Cripple Creek, the road branched in several directions, but the Shelf Road served as the main trail for many years. Originally used by Native Americans and later by fur trappers, Shelf Road was the quickest way to the Cripple Creek District from Canon City. The Canon City & Cripple Creek Toll Road was established along Shelf Road in 1891. The road was so named after Canon City business leaders attempted to improve the old trail by blasting literal shelves out of the canyon walls in 1892. Despite its precarious curves, the improved road could accommodate the first stage lines of David Wood and John Montgomery Kuykendall.

When Wood's line went under, Kuykendall established his own monopoly with more comfortable and modern Caulkin stagecoaches and low rates. Two stage stops, Marigold and Eldred, provided fresh horses, food, and supplies. Eldred in particular was not much more than a couple of small one-room log cabins, but promised hot meals and cool drinks to travelers. Marigold provided travelers with a post office from October 31, 1895 to 1902. Over time, a railroad company and

A group of men pose in front of Victor's St. James Hotel in April 1894. Within a few months, Victor would be the first district town to have not one, but two railroads. (Courtesy Cipple Creek District Museum.)

two trolley companies considered utilizing the Shelf Road. Wisely, those thoughts of extending tracks up the narrow roadbed were quickly dismissed. From 1892 to 1897, Gideon Thomas and his two sons established a freight route via the Shelf Road and other area trails.

A much lesser known and older route from the south was the Beaver Creek trail that wound its way up from the Florence suburb of Penrose. Interestingly, Penrose appears originally to have been named Fremont, but its actual relation to Fremont in the Cripple Creek District is unknown. The Beaver Creek post office was first established way back in 1862 and functioned until 1874. The post office of Toof replaced it in 1881, and in 1883 the name was changed back to Beaver Creek. Then in 1902, the name was shortened to Beaver. Very little is known about these communities. What is known is that a winding trail, located east of Phantom Canyon and Shelf Road, skirted the creek and eventually came out near Victor. Why the trail never gained more popularity is unknown.

Other ways of getting to Cripple Creek included the Holbert or Howbert Trail (possibly originating near Lake George), the High Park Trail that traversed much of today's High Park Road, and the Bear Creek Road from Colorado Springs. The toll road from Divide, over which the Midland Terminal would later lay its tracks, passed through the station of Murphy. Originally known as Tracy, Murphy was located along Tracy Hill. Throughout the life of the Midland Terminal, railroad engineers used Murphy as a landmark along the trip to and from the Cripple Creek District. Later, a quarry would be established near the station.

The easiest and most popular wagon route to the Cripple Creek District was the road from Florissant. In March of 1892, there were two stage lines running from Florissant to Fremont: the Hundley Stage Line and the Montgomery Stage Line. In May, the Welty brothers introduced a third stage line. Of the three, Hundley's Stage Line appears to have been most popular since it ran all the way from Colorado Springs. Whether passengers rode the stage from the Springs or took the Midland Railroad to Florissant, the two-hour trip to Cripple Creek from Florissant cost a whopping $10. Hundley's Concord coaches were first class, often pulled by six or more horses. It was said that the company transported as much as 4 tons of freight along the Florissant Road in a single day.

But even the less frightening stage roads were bumpy, long, and uncomfortable. The trip along Shelf Road alone took two to four hours, depending on the direction of travel. Sometimes passengers had to disembark in order to push the coach through mud or assist in maneuvering it around rocks and narrow bends in the road. Winter storms made the trips dangerous and unbearable. Rumors of railroads coming to the Cripple Creek District began to circulate. A variety of railroads were already making regular stops in Colorado Springs. Among them were General William Jackson Palmer's Denver & Rio Grande, as well as the Missouri Pacific, the Rock Island, and the Santa Fe Railroad lines. There was also the Colorado Midland, which had been chugging regularly up Ute Pass since the 1880s.

Despite establishing a freight office on Bennett Avenue in Cripple Creek as early as 1892, the Midland was not the first railroad in the Cripple Creek District, nor was it the first railroad to reach Cripple Creek. Its presence, however,

John Hundley's Concord stagecoaches and ample horsepower almost guaranteed a safe trip for both passengers and freight. (Courtesy Cripple Creek District Museum.)

combined with the steep and perilous roads from Canon City, was enough to discourage the Denver & Rio Grande Railroad from attempting to build a railroad to the district. The Colorado Midland had more pull than just a freight office in Cripple Creek. It was also a division of the Santa Fe Railroad, one of the Denver & Rio Grande's toughest competitors. But unfortunately, the Midland was also fraught with dilemmas.

For one thing, the Midland's general manager Harry Collbran, as well as supporters Irving Howbert and W.K. Gillett, were having a hard time convincing the Santa Fe to build. The threesome finally joined up with Harlan Lillibridge, whose own dream of building a narrow-gauge railroad up the Cheyenne Toll Road had failed to come to fruition. Together, the men worked to raise $100,000 and the Midland Terminal Railroad was born. Initially, the Midland Terminal was meant to be a narrow-gauge railroad. As the magnitude of the coming gold rush hit, however, arguments sprouted over the feasibility of 24-inch tracks and small railroad cars versus the larger cars of a standard gauge railroad. Throughout 1892 and much of 1893, construction was at a standstill.

In the meantime, the Florence & Cripple Creek Railroad (F&CC) was being constructed along what was originally known as Ute Canyon between Victor and the town of Florence, located some 35 miles south. Later, this canyon would be named Eight Mile Canyon and, finally, Phantom Canyon. Headed by Florence merchant James A. McCandless, engineers first began surveying the canyon as early as 1891. In March of 1892, the Florence Free Road was established by Thomas Robinson. The road was meant to eventually reach the Wyoming state border. No sooner had the Salaman Stage Line debuted on the Florence Free

One of several F&CC depots is visible in the lower left of this undated photograph of Goldfield. (Courtesy Cripple Creek District Museum.)

Road, then plans began for the Florence and Cripple Creek State Line Railroad. A map of the new railroad was filed in May of 1892, but the company was later reformed as the Florence & Cripple Creek Railroad.

The F&CC was financed by Denver & Rio Grande Railroad magnate David Moffat, and the company was incorporated in April of 1893. Construction of the railroad commenced in about December of 1893, just as the Midland Terminal reached the toll station of Midland. The first Midland Terminal depot was constructed there. To the south, the Clough and Davidson Construction Company had already plowed a toll road along Oil Creek. Today, this road is known locally as the Four Mile Cut-off.

From Midland, passengers transferred to stagecoaches bound for Cripple Creek. As the tracks were laid, more small camps were erected for railroad workers. Later, many of these same camps, such as the tiny place of Waters, functioned as railroad stops for passenger pickup or water stops. Waters was actually named for Jessie Waters, a superintendent of the Midland Terminal. It was said that Waters played an integral part in the race between the Midland Terminal and the F&CC to reach Cripple Creek. Upon learning the F&CC had procured a permit to lay their tracks along Fifth Street, Waters set about getting the rival crew drunk on whiskey. The minute work ceased, Waters scrambled to get an injunction and prevented the F&CC from laying their tracks in the Midland Terminal's path. Ever grateful, the Midland Terminal named its only tunnel after Waters and put him up in a fine home on Silver Street in Cripple Creek. Unfortunately, Waters was killed on the railroad in 1914. In later years, this same tunnel became known as the "Little Ike," a parody of the Eisenhower tunnel near Denver.

In their time, settlements like Waters served as important stops along the railroad. Most of these place names no longer exist at all. One community in particular, however, survived to blossom into a bona fide railroad town. This was Gillett, housed in an expansive meadow just 7 miles from Waters to the west and about 4 miles from Cripple Creek. Today, the average passerby would never know this quiet place once housed a town populated with 1,200 people, a casino, and even a racetrack. The town housed miners and railroad employees, as well as workers at some nearby mills. Gillett was first settled in 1893 and initially was called Cripple City.

When it was platted in July 1894, the new town was renamed for W.K. Gillett, an official on the Midland Terminal who in fact had a lot to do with building the railroad. This enterprising businessman would later become known as the builder of the fabulous National Hotel in Cripple Creek. In Gillett, Parker Street was the main drag and may have been named for J.M. Parker, president of Cripple Creek's First National Bank. Gillett prided itself for having the only other bank outside of Cripple Creek and Victor. Fine, false-fronted wooden buildings lined Parker Street, with aspen trees added for accent.

In August of 1895, Gillett would gain notoriety when the town was the site of the only "legal" bullfight ever officially recorded in the United States. Joe Wolfe of Cripple Creek's prestigious Palace Hotel and a former Wild West performer named "Arizona Charlie" Meadows acted as promoters, boisterously naming their project the Joe Wolfe Grand National Spanish Bull Fight Company. The pair borrowed $5,000, built a 5,000-seat amphitheater at Tutt and Penrose's racetrack, and even imported matadors from Mexico. Tickets and posters were printed in anticipation of the event, which was slated to take place on August 24, 25, and 26.

About 3,000 people attended the first day of the fights, despite the Colorado Springs *Gazette*'s article which labeled the event as inhumane:

> If it be illegal to import bulls for fighting at the Atlanta Exposition, surely it must be illegal to import them across the border for fighting at the Gillett Exposition. Here is a chance for Francis Hill of the Humane Society to write to the Secretary of the Treasury, informing him that it is proposed to import bulls for the same purpose of fighting and . . . keep them out of El Paso County.

In the end, the bulls that were supposed to be imported from Mexico were prevented from entering the United States at the Texas border. Wolfe and Meadows ended up using common local bulls, whose complacent natures were hardly conducive to those of their feistier Mexican counterparts. What was intended to be an exciting event turned into a senseless, slow, and cruel death for the animals. Americans didn't care for the grisly killings as much as the promoters thought they would. Less than 300 people showed for the fight on the second day, opting instead to watch as the Midland Terminal reached the town of Anaconda. Wolfe and Meadows were arrested after canceling the fight for the third day. The one saving grace was that meat from the slaughtered bulls was distributed among the city's poor.

The Midland Terminal Railroad tracks passed right through Gillett, with the train making its debut there on Independence Day in 1894. The new railroad did much to support Gillett's namesake town. There were also smelters and reduction mills, such as the Beaver Park Stamp Mill, which employed 100 men and maintained its own small camp. Although numerous diggings on the outskirts of town turned up nothing, two mines contributed employment and a little gold ore. They were the Lincoln (alternately known as the Lincoln & Gibbons) and the King of Diamonds.

Despite its seeming lack of big industry, Gillett appears to have been a test market for many area millionaires. The Woods brothers of Victor were partial owners of the Golden Crescent Water and Light Company at Gillett. Spencer Penrose and Charles Tutt, both wealthy men of Utah, Cripple Creek, and Colorado Springs, built their own racetrack and gambling casino. This last entity could be one reason why Gillett became known as the Cripple Creek District's "bachelor town."

Just before the Midland Terminal reached Gillett, the F&CC successfully reached Victor and traveled on through Anaconda. It was truly a victorious day when the first F&CC train reached Cripple Creek. Incidentally, most reports claim the F&CC first steamed into Cripple Creek on July 1, 1894. In actuality, construction crews had managed to finish the track the day before, June 30. An engine and eight construction cars had reached an area just a half mile outside of town. When the crew finished the track around 11 a.m., they moved the train to the end of the track and blew the whistle several times. Townspeople swarmed the train and admired the newly laid tracks, but the official inauguration was not held until the next day. There was much celebration as nearly the whole town turned out to see the event. In the morning, several passengers boarded the train for its return trip.

Unfortunately, fate dealt the new railroad a crooked hand. Shortly after leaving Cripple Creek on the morning of July 2, the baggage car and both coaches of the train derailed as they chugged through Anaconda between Cripple Creek and Victor. Train cars lay like forgotten toys along the hillside, yielding 1 fatality (W.G. Milner of Denver) and 21 injuries. The mess was quickly cleaned up, the track fixed, and the F&CC chugged into history with that incident the only one to ever occur in its history—in the district, anyway.

Despite the tragedy, the F&CC recovered quickly. Soon there were towns springing up right next to the tracks and the number of depots in the district grew. Just outside of Florence, the railroad chugged through the whistle stops of Cyanide and Vesta Junction before proceeding across today's Highway 50 and up Phantom Canyon. The next stop north of today's Highway 50 was Oro Junta, followed by Cramer, Alabaster (later known as Russell), and McCourt. The last

The bullfight at Gillett was both a scandal and a scam that is still widely talked about today. Few were in attendance on the last day, as an obviously domesticated Hereford bull wandered into the ring. (Courtesy Mazzulla Collection, Cripple Creek District Museum.)

Photos of the first F&CC Railroad train into Cripple Creek are dated July 1; in actuality, the train arrived the day before. (Courtesy Cripple Creek District Museum.)

town's founder was actually Peter McCourt, brother to the silver millionairess Elizabeth "Baby Doe" Tabor.

The saga of the Tabor family is well known Colorado history. Upon arriving in Central City as the restless wife of a miner, Baby Doe took a trip by herself to Leadville, where she met and eventually married silver millionaire Horace Tabor in 1882. Consequently, the couple bestowed Peter McCourt the job of managing the Tabor Grand Opera House in Denver. His brother Philip was hired as treasurer. When the Tabors lost everything during the silver crash of 1893, only Peter appears to have been prepared. The closing of the opera house put him out of a job, but he had wisely saved his money. Baby Doe appealed to Peter to help the falling Tabor empire, but Peter was unsympathetic. "I haven't any money to spare," he told her, "and even if I could, you'd only throw it away on some silly extravagance."

Probably to escape the woes and shame of his sister, Peter decided to check out the Cripple Creek boom. He arrived in about 1893 and was immediately inaugurated into the Cripple Creek Elks Lodge. The move is not mentioned in most Tabor biographies and information about Peter's correspondence with the family is scant. It is known, however, that Peter soon developed an interest in the F&CC.

Within the year, McCourt established a small railroad station, supplemented by a nearby quartz mine staked by himself along with his brother Philip, C.A. Bass of Denver, and Dr. John Whiting of Cripple Creek. Plans were in the making to erect a small stamp mill. McCourt Camp was located at an altitude of 6,483 feet, situated 13 miles from Florence and 20 miles from Cripple Creek. Other claims were staked as well, mostly in the interest of gaining water rights. The

F&CC tracks had passed McCourt by March of 1894. Within a few months, they extended as far as Wilbur and regular passenger service began. Upon arriving at Wilbur, passengers were transferred to a stage for the remainder of their trip to the Cripple Creek District. Wilbur actually numbered 60 souls and quickly grew to include a post office, school, and a saloon.

The flood, as well as the harsh lifestyle at McCourt, finally proved too much for Peter McCourt. From all indications, he closed up his Western Union telegraph office, forgot about his claims, and returned to Denver where he leased the Broadway Theater, which he ran very successfully for many years. Philip apparently tired of riding his brother's coat tails and eventually pursued a career as a professional gambler.

Little else is known about McCourt. Some years later, a prospector near the camp was delighted to find good ore in Ute Creek. It was only after he staked his claim that he discovered the ore was the result of a long ago derailment of the railroad, during which the ore spilled into the stream. There is nothing to suggest Peter ever returned to Cripple Creek, but he did continue to make the occasional headline. After Horace Tabor died in poverty in 1899, Peter was known to send money to Baby Doe's daughters, Elizabeth and Silver. When Elizabeth tired of life at the Tabor's depleted Matchless Mine in Leadville, Peter willingly paid her way back to the family homeland of Oshkosh, Wisconsin. In 1925, he also paid for Silver's funeral after she died of an accidental scalding. When he passed away, Peter included Baby Doe in his will, but she refused the bequest. Her comment at the time was probably more prophetic than she knew. "Living, he forgot me when misfortune came;" she once wrote, "dead, he can give me nothing."

On the F&CC tracks, McCourt was followed by Robinson, later known as Adelaide and then Comstock. Few other people lived in the area, so passenger pickup was scarce at Adelaide. The next stop was Wilders, then Glenbrook. For a short time, a community called Dunnville existed after prospectors found gold ore at Glenbrook. Nothing came of the ore samples, however, and the tent colony moved on within two days. Just up the track was Wilbur, later known as Mosher. At the turn of the century, 60 people were living at Wilbur, which boasted a school and even a saloon. The post office at Wilbur operated from September 1894 to July 1913. The last stop before Victor was Alta Vista, whose tiny depot was later saved and now serves as a welcome center in Victor.

The Midland Terminal boys might have snickered at the F&CC's unfortunate wreck just a day after its debut in Cripple Creek. While it may be said the F&CC beat the Midland Terminal to Cripple Creek, however, the idea of an actual race would have been impossible anyway. From Gillett to Cripple Creek, there is a 750-foot drop in altitude over the last 2 miles coming into town. To snake a railroad track, standard gauge or otherwise, down the precarious Tenderfoot Hill above town would have required a miracle. Hence, the Midland Terminal continued its trek past the town of Gillett and towards the city of Victor. The railroad reached the town of Grassy, later called Cameron, in the autumn of 1894 and built a small depot there before continuing on to Independence.

It was there that the Midland crew encountered the first of more than one trouble regarding right-of-ways. Sylvester Yeoman, a partner in the Black Wonder Mine, took exception to the Midland's 50-foot right-of-way through his claim. Ultimately Yeoman was paid $125 in damages, but the presence of his cabin on the Black Wonder would force the Midland tracks to swerve around a sharp curve. In a contest of wills, chief engineer Richard Newell Jr. disembarked from the train one day in December of 1894 with a court order to move the cabin or tear it down.

As Newell approached the cabin, the door opened and one of three men inside fired a rifle directly into Newell's chest. He died almost instantly. Aaron W. Van Houten, an alleged fugitive from Aspen who was merely using the cabin to work some claims nearby, was arrested for the murder. Yeoman and the other two men from the cabin were charged as accessories to the crime. The cabin was torn down shortly after. Construction continued on the railroad and the Midland Terminal reached Victor in late December.

Frontier justice was indeed blatant in those early days. Settlers who had arrived well before the railroads often felt as thought their territory was being invaded.

Adelaide was located just a short distance up the F&CC Railroad tracks from McCourt. Extra "helper" engines were kept on hand at Adelaide to help push the trains up the last steep grade into the district. At the tiny train station of Alta Vista, the engines were turned around to head back down to Adelaide. (Courtesy Cripple Creek District Museum.)

The F&CC Railroad suffered its first—and only—wreck in the district during its second day of operation. (Courtesy Cripple Creek District Museum.)

One camp that did not experience this problem was Love, the last community to officially debut in the Cripple Creek District during 1894. Alternately called Beaver Park, Love was named for a nearby rancher's spread, located at the extreme east end of the district. Although small, the community supported a school and a cemetery, as well as a store and a post office beginning in December. Most members of the community were ranchers, with the occasional miner taking up residence as well. Love, however, was remote enough that members of outlaw Butch Cassidy's notorious Wild Bunch also felt secure in procuring a hideout there shortly after the community was founded.

The good people at Love, as well as the outlaws, had few worries about their village becoming a booming metropolis. By January of 1895, any interest in the tiny community shifted as folks began flocking to the next big town of the Cripple Creek District, Goldfield. The town was platted that month, with its post office opening in May. Today, Goldfield is the smallest and only other surviving town in the district besides Cripple Creek and Victor. The city lies at an altitude of 9,903 feet on the outskirts of Montgomery Gulch, better known now as the Vindicator Valley. To the east is Big Bull Mountain. To the west is the former town of Independence, surrounded by the ghost mines of Teresa, the Golden Cycle, the Portland #1 and #2, the Findley, the Independence, and the Vindicator.

Goldfield's suburbs included Bull Hill, a small camp on Bull Mountain northwest of town, and Eagle Junction near the Eagle Sampler Mine above Goldfield. Originally, James Doyle and J.F. "Jimmy" Burns, owners of the Portland Mine, formed the Gold Knob Mining and Townsite Company. Later, the name was changed to Goldfield, probably because nobody wanted to live in a town called Gold Knob. Lots at Goldfield started at $25 each. Referred to as the "City of Homes," Goldfield was a family town. Unlike other district towns, Goldfield's citizens were far more interested in establishing schools and churches than saloons.

Two newspapers, the *Goldfield Gazette* and the *Goldfield Times*, set about reporting the issues at hand, and they didn't have to wait long. The infamous labor strike of 1894 arrived about the same time as Goldfield. Not ironically, all of Goldfield's town officials belonged to the Western Federation of Miners Union. The most prominent union man in Goldfield was its first mayor, District Judge John Easter. The first mayor lost no time in establishing a fire department and hired a city physician at $300 per year. Goldfield even had a "pest house" for confining those with contagious diseases such as tuberculosis. The town made its business clear with the firing of Albert Pheasants, a pest house attendant who showed up for work inebriated.

Saloons, businesses, and even dogs were dutifully licensed, and there were strict ordinances against prostitution in Goldfield. Portland, Independence, and Victor Avenue were three of the main streets. A town engineer maintained these and other roads for $10 per day. So efficient was the new town that one source says Goldfield already had a population of 2,191 by the end of its first year. This figure may include the town of Independence, however, which was already being governed by Goldfield. The Midland Terminal tracks, other railroads, as well as the F&CC, divided the two cities.

In spite of its growing success, the F&CC was not without its problems. In March of 1895, train service was delayed when five members of Victor's infamous Crumley Gang robbed the train between Victor and Alta Vista. Sherman Crumley escaped prosecution, but four men were sentenced to the Canon City State Penitentiary for the deed. One or two more robberies took place in later years, but a quick getaway wasn't easy for the robbers, who usually lived in communities close to the railroad. For one thing, the narrow walls of Phantom Canyon made it hard to escape on anything other than foot. Also, the population was continuously growing. There were always too many witnesses.

The railroad was given a brief reprieve in April with the premiere of the town of Elkton, located halfway between Victor and Cripple Creek. The town was founded by William Shemwell, a former blacksmith from Colorado Springs who staked the Elkton Mine. Both the mine and the town were named for a pair of elk antlers found lying on the ground. By 1900, there were 200 people at Elkton, which soon grew to absorb the residents of Arequa and nearby Beacon Hill.

The F&CC had barely enough time to erect its newest depot at Elkton when a flood washed out a good bit of the railroad in July or August of 1895. The southbound train had just passed through Glenbrook when the flash flood came crashing around the corner behind the train. The train raced the flood for the remaining 13 miles to Russell. Behind the train, stations, bridges, and tracks were washed out. At Adelaide, a total of six people—Mrs. Carr and Lee Tracey of the Great Elk Hotel, a boarder named Watson, and three employees of the F&CC—

drowned in the flood waters. Nearly 10 miles of track were ruined. The railroad managed to repair the damage at a cost of $1 million and Adelaide was moved up to the present road.

Midland Terminal crew workers had plenty of time to speculate about the F&CC's troubles as they toiled to lay tracks to Elkton and beyond. There is little doubt that citizens and railroad employees alike looked forward to the tracks reaching their ultimate destination, Cripple Creek. In anticipation of the historic event, the railroad's investors worked with the city to establish what would be the fanciest and largest Midland Terminal Depot in the district. The two entities achieved this goal in October of 1895, when the city of Cripple Creek established an ordinance to deed permanent use of Bennett Avenue's east end to the depot.

In December of 1895, the Midland Terminal finally reached Cripple Creek. By then, the district had thus far mined more than $8 million in gold, surpassing the profits and notoriety of California's gold boom of 1849. Cripple Creek was literally booming as buildings flew up and people poured into the district. The city was striving harder than ever to be first class and its citizens worked at ignoring

The school at Love did not suffer for lack of students. Among the children pictured here are Ceylon Stumpf, whose father built one of the first cabins in the district, and Frankie Ferguson, later a mayor of Cripple Creek and the namesake of the city's library. (Courtesy Cripple Creek District Museum.)

A year before this photo was taken in 1897, Goldfield was already growing to become the third largest city in the district. (Courtesy Cripple Creek District Museum.)

such unpleasant aspects as Myers Avenue, where upwards of 300 prostitutes flourished on any given day. Soon, respectable folks didn't want to be associated with Myers Avenue, even though a good number of them lived on it. To alleviate further embarrassment, Myers Avenue from about the middle of Third Street and west to the city limits was renamed Masonic Avenue.

These formal attempts at establishing a more refined culture in the district went largely unnoticed by newcomers. By 1896, Goldfield alone had a population of 1,000. The town elected its second marshal, Allen Combs. Apparently, the duties of being town marshal needed definition; the city put forth an ordinance with Combs's appointment, stating the town marshal could be replaced if found too drunk to work. A marshal who was adept at his duties was becoming important. Goldfield had grown to include two assayers, an attorney, two boarding houses, one dentist, three groceries, one hotel, two meat markets, three doctors, and three saloons. A reservoir made use of several natural springs in the area. Fire hydrants were installed on every corner. Ditches, covered with wooden sidewalks, paralleled each street so homes were amply supplied with water. Goldfield boasted more sidewalks than any other town in the district.

Goldfield was not the only town experiencing massive growth. Gillett had overcome its embarrassing bullfight incident. Now, two daily trains stopped at the attractive wooden railroad station, their passengers having a pick of four different newspapers to read on the trip to or from Cripple Creek: the *Gillett Forum*, the *Gillett Advertiser*, the *Sunday Chronicle*, and the *Gillett Gazette*. (All of the newspapers folded within a year, the exception being the *Forum*, which lasted until 1905.) A telegraph office was also available at the train station. Other modern amenities included fire hydrants, 41 assay offices, 91 attorneys, 14 saloons, 3 dance halls, and a jail. In addition, there were rumored to be several stills hidden in the hills, which lasted well through Prohibition. The Beaver Park Land Company was selling lots for $25 to $100 and had local offices in Cripple Creek, Colorado Springs, Pueblo, and Denver. Other offices were located as far away as Chicago and Detroit. The land company even left room for a cemetery, which was accessed by a road leading from Father Volpe's Catholic Church.

Over in Altman, the population in 1896 was still 1,000. By the following year, the figure had doubled. Altman was recovering from the labor wars and grew to include several structures scattered along the hillsides around town. Main, Baldwin, and Brown Streets appear to be the main thoroughfares, cross sectioned by First, Second, and Third Streets. Business buildings were of the wooden, false-fronted variety. Servicing the citizens were a drugstore, assayer, bakery, cobbler, hotel, two restaurants, two liveries, two physicians, two churches, four barbers, four groceries, and five merchandise stores. Eight boarding houses served as homes to the transient miner population. Six saloons served thirsty miners at all hours of the day and night. They included the Thirst Parlor, The Mint, The Silver Dollar, and the Monte Carlo.

The presence of so many taverns in this remote spot resulted in some wild nights in the town of Altman. Bare-knuckled boxing took place on a regular basis. An undertaker allegedly offered to give group rates for funerals on Saturdays. After a justice of the peace from nearby Anaconda was assaulted in Altman, the latter dutifully employed a marshal. The first was Mike McKinnon, who allegedly died in a gunfight with six Texans—but not before he killed all six outlaws. McKinnon was followed by Jack Kelly, who once battled it out with gangster "General" Jack Smith. The latter was killed after firing a shot at Kelly that strayed and killed another gangster.

Below Altman, Victor was having little trouble living up to its nickname as the "City of Mines." Back in 1894, the Woods brothers had been excavating their new Victor Hotel when construction workers hit a particularly rich vein of gold. Plans for the hotel were quickly scrapped as the Woods staked the Gold Coin Mine right in the middle of town. Within a few years, the Woods had constructed the Victor Hotel in another spot. They also built the elite Gold Coin Club directly across from the Gold Coin Mine. The club served two purposes. Miners at the Gold Coin had exclusive use of a bar, pool tables, and other forms of recreation at the club. At the same time, the Woods could keep a close eye on their employees, requiring them to shower at the club and searching their clothing to prevent theft of their precious gold.

For many years, the Woods reigned supreme in Victor, which grew to absorb Lawrence as well as the mining suburbs of Los Angeles at the Los Angeles Mine and Hollywood, named after saloon owner Frank Hollywood. Other suburbs included Dutchtown, south of Lawrence; the railroad junction of Dyer; Portland at the Portland Mine; and Strong's Camp, located at Sam Strong's mine. It was not at all unusual by this time to see camps surrounding working mines or for various nationalities to establish their own communities.

Still, other smaller camps attempted to establish post offices during the year 1896 but failed. These included the hamlets of Signal in May, Horace in June, and Seward in August. One other failed camp bears mention. The Bare Hills, located 10 miles southwest of Cripple Creek, was also known as Bare Hill City as early as 1894. A few mines were established nearby and Gideon Thomas hauled supplies between there and Victor possibly via Shelf Road. In 1896, Bare Hills became known as Furrow City. The new "town" was promoted as being located on the same gold belt as the Cripple Creek District. In November of 1897, the Bare Hills Road was completed. Sponsored by the Cripple Creek Chamber of Commerce, the new road ran south from town, passing over the saddle south of Mt. Pisgah to Four Mile Creek. Unfortunately, only a few lots were sold at Furrow City before folks caught on and refused to buy the false claims of certain wealth.

By 1896, Victor was growing to become the second largest city in the Cripple Creek District and the fifth largest city in the state. (Courtesy Cripple Creek District Museum.)

5. BURNING MEMORIES
(1896–1899)

In the days before smoke alarms, fire frequently signified the demise of many a mining town. Most boom town buildings were erected with alarming speed, and the lack of such barriers as building permits and codes gave free rein to would-be architects. Hence, Cripple Creek resembled the average gold mining town with the usual assortment of ramshackle wood buildings and false fronts. There was a healthy tent population as well, scattered on lots, in back alleys, between buildings, and on the hillsides around town. An estimated 15,000 people were calling the place home.

Within four days during April of 1896, two separate fires burned down about half of Cripple Creek. The young mining camp had already suffered another fire in April of 1892, when it lost seven buildings on Bennett Avenue. In that case, a dance hall girl by the name of Lutie Cook was credited with saving two small children who were trapped on the second floor of the Arcade Restaurant. The fearless harlot handed the children down from the window before escaping from the flames herself. On April 25, 1896, yet another dance hall girl turned out to be the villain in the first of two devastating fires. Her name was Jennie LaRue and, before the end of the month, hers became a household name across the nation as the vixen who started the fire of Cripple Creek.

There had not been substantial snow in the district for two weeks, but a slight dusting the night before had left the streets muddy. Except for the gusty winds, which are typical of April, it was a nice day. The city of Cripple Creek had every confidence in its fire department, which consisted of a regularly trained team of firemen, 175 volunteers, 3 hose carts, a hook-and-ladder truck, and a chemical engine. All were hand drawn, yet seemingly capable of controlling even the most threatening blaze. The town's water system included brand new fire hydrants and fire alarm boxes on every street. Just that morning, the Saturday edition of the *Cripple Creek Morning Times* had reported, "Our splendid system of water works and well-disciplined firemen make it possible to control and extinguish the most serious conflagration possible; henceforth our citizens can be free of this terror."

Enter the lone figure of a man making his way down Third Street and onto Myers Avenue around noon. The city-dressed dude was muttering something about the woman who stole his money as he continued up Myers and turned in at the Central Dance Hall. From there, the man made his way up to Jennie LaRue's second-floor room, where the dance hall girl stood ironing near a gasoline stove. Her task was interrupted by the angry visitor, demanding to know where his money was. In turn, she was upset because he missed a date with her. The two began to argue, then to fight. In the mayhem, the stove overturned, quickly igniting the floor with spreading flames.

The incredible fire that followed this incident in 1896 would give anyone the fantods. The fire burned over $1 million in buildings and belongings. And at the root of it all was the hapless Jennie LaRue. Newspapers as far away as Denver spewed the woman's name forth in a heartbeat, but most accounts leave the name of her fightin' man out. Over the years, various sources have narrowed the suspects down to three. One is an unnamed bartender from the Topic Theatre. Another is a Mr. Jones, who ran the lunch counter at the Central. But the third suspect is most likely our man. He's that fellow with the funny name, Otto Floto.

Otto Clement Floto was born in Cincinnati around 1863. After attending a Jesuit school in Dayton, he did some sports writing in Chicago before drifting west. The 1896 Cripple Creek city directory lists Floto as the manager of the Cripple Creek Bill Posting Company. The 22-year-old actually had many occupations, if each report about him is to be believed. Several sources say he was a bartender. Author Marshal Sprague states Floto managed the Butte Opera House, and his obituary touts him as a friend and advisor to world-famous boxer Jack Dempsey during the latter's youth in Cripple Creek.

As for Jennie LaRue, city directories fail to acknowledge her presence in Cripple Creek at all. In fact, of 900 prostitutes and dance hall floozies documented in the Cripple Creek District, Jennie and her possible aliases have yet to be found. Yet, in Cripple Creek she was on the day of that fire. Incidentally, neither Jennie nor her mysterious consort appear to have been held lawfully responsible for the fire.

Perhaps the largest clue to Jennie LaRue's mystery man lies in a marriage certificate filed at the El Paso County courthouse. Dated October 20, 1896, the document reveals the marriage of Otto C. Floto to one Jennie Ried. If the lovely Ms. LaRue was true to her profession and sported an alias, Ried could have been her legal surname. Whomever Jennie really was, she and Otto left town within months of their marriage.

Floto next surfaced in Carson City, Nevada in February of 1897. At a boxing match between Gentleman Jim Corbett and Ruby Bob Fitzsimmons, Floto met Harry Tammen, publisher of the *Denver Post*. Tammen wanted to use Otto's delightful surname for a performing circus act the *Post* owned and hired Floto to report on sporting events. "Floto admitted when he took the job that he couldn't write," Tammen later recalled, "and the truth of the matter is I hired him because he had the most beautiful name in the world. It fascinated me . . . "

Myers Avenue grew considerably in both size and reputation between the time this photo was taken in 1892 and the first fire on April 25, 1896. (Courtesy Grace L. Faus Collection, Cripple Creek District Museum.)

Tammen found even more uses for Otto's unique name, such as using it to promote an all new performing act. Shortly after Floto's Dog & Pony Show was organized, Otto and Jennie parted ways. Jennie disappeared. Floto continued writing for the *Post*, becoming one of the most prominent sportswriters in America for his time. By 1905, the Floto Dog & Pony Show had blossomed into the Sells-Floto Circus. While traveling with the circus, Floto met and married a bareback rider named Kitty Kruger. The two were married in Denver in 1906 and remained together throughout Floto's life. Four years later, Floto made sporting editor at the *Post*. Floto's marriage to Kitty Kruger was set in stone, or so it seemed.

In later years, Floto's associates would remember him as somewhat of a vain ladies' man, who insisted on using a much more youthful photo of himself to illustrate his column. Floto's passion for pretty girls was no secret around the office. A co-worker recalled the time Floto was held up by business. The young lady who had appeared around quitting time grew impatient waiting for the writing Romeo and left. In fact, Floto's charisma may have been lost on the girl; he reportedly weighed 250 pounds at one time. Author Gene Fowler, however, remembered Floto fondly as "lovable, generous and loyal."

When Otto Floto died of epilepsy at the youthful age of 66, the *Denver Post* ran his extensive obituary on the front page. It was a fitting reward for 32 years of service for that newspaper. He left behind no children, only Kitty and his brother William, but a handful of notable sports figures sent condolences. Among them was Jack Dempsey. In its own way, it was a last salute to Otto Floto's Cripple Creek beginnings and his link to the infamous fires.

Cripple Creek's fire on April 25, 1896 destroyed much of Myers Avenue but only a few business blocks on Bennett Avenue. (Courtesy Cripple Creek District Museum.)

Floto was hardly thinking of his future that fateful day in Jennie LaRue's room, however. He and Jennie managed to escape, but so quick was the resulting inferno that some of the bawdy girls on the third floor were forced to escape by rope. By that time, folks were gathering on the streets to watch the flames as the alarm boxes were pulled and the fire department rushed to the scene. As it happened, Cripple Creek was in between fire chiefs and there was no one present to coordinate the operation. To make matters worse, the new fire hydrant connections were too small to fit the hoses. Even before water could be turned on the Central Dance Hall, wind spread the fire to the Union Dance Hall and Carey's Second-Hand store on either side. Once the hoses were hooked up, weak water pressure necessitated disconnecting some of them. A hose break caused another delay of 10 to 15 minutes. Finally, a strong stream of water doused the flames for the next half hour. But again, the water pressure weakened due to the number of hydrants operating.

Meanwhile, flames engulfed the two-story Topic Theatre, which burned quickly. As the roof caught fire, strong winds fanned the embers onto other buildings. The inferno spread south to Warren Avenue and north via Third, Fourth, and Fifth Streets. Fifty buildings blazed at once on Myers Avenue as the fire jumped across the alley and began setting to the backs of buildings on Bennett. Along the front of Bennett, shop owners scurried to carry their goods outside before the fire engulfed their stores.

Narrow escapes from death or injury were numerous as other residents fled just ahead of the flames. The overall result was a mass of flaming walls as the streets teemed with humanity and belongings. The fire traveled north as far as

Eaton Avenue, where firemen used the remaining water to confine the edges of the burning area. To keep the fire from moving westward, buildings on the east side of Third between Myers and Bennett were blown up with dynamite. While the total number of injuries will probably never be known, the worst casualties appeared to be a fireman whose leg was blown off and two men who suffered head injuries.

Indeed, Cripple Creek lost much of its detested red light district, but also a number of businesses in the 300 block of Bennett and Carr Avenues. Only by dynamiting buildings along Third Street were firemen able to stop the flames from spreading beyond the 30 acres already burned. Almost every building on Bennett between Third and Fourth Streets was destroyed. Johnny Nolon's saloon totaled the highest loss in town. Also gone were the Cripple Creek Mining Exchange, the First National Bank, and the post office with 25,000 pieces of undelivered mail. More than 30 homes on Carr and Eaton were destroyed as well.

In the end, up to 3,600 people were left homeless by the fire, but the town recovered surprisingly fast. Telegraph and telephone service was restored within an hour and temporary housing was quickly provided as far away as Victor, Florence, and Colorado Springs. Many stores and businesses were able to reopen quickly. The town grew quiet as night fell. Despite orders to close all saloons, Joe Finley and George Jordan reopened the My Friend Saloon in a tent on Myers and were serving drinks by evening. The *Cripple Creek Times* announced it had relocated to Golden Avenue and would publish as usual on Sunday morning. City employees received word their paychecks would be issued the following day.

By the time of Cripple Creek's second fire on Wednesday, April 29, the city was recovering well. Firemen were hauling the last of the debris and dumping it in abandoned prospect holes when a maid at the Portland Hotel allegedly spilled a pot of grease onto a lit stove. Built in 1892 as the Windsor Hotel, the Portland had become rundown since its glory days and was quickly engulfed in flames. Its owner L.J. Moynahan later asserted the blaze was intentionally set by a renter, Mr. Brewer. Moynahan stated Mr. Brewer carried high insurance due to expire May 1. Whether Brewer was ever held responsible for this charge is lost to history.

As before, the grease fire quickly developed into a raging inferno. Again, stiff winds fed the blaze, which spread with alarming quickness. The Portland collapsed as more buildings caught fire. Panicking in the wake of yet another fire, people piled wagons, carts, clothes, furniture, whiskey barrels, and other goods in the streets. Women and children were directed to run up to the reservoir and meet their families there.

This time, the already depleted water supply ran out within an hour. Caches of dynamite blew up unexpectedly. Then the boilers at the Palace Hotel exploded, sending flames 100 feet into the air. Next, 700 pounds of dynamite stored at the Harder Grocery Store on Myers exploded. Buildings such as N.O. Johnson's, which survived the first fire, were lost as the blaze passed over the site a second time. Dynamite was used once more, but to no avail. People in other district towns some 3 to 6 miles away reported hearing the blasts and the roar of the flames. Fifteen city blocks, including the rest of Bennett Avenue and as far north as Golden, were soon burning hopelessly out of control.

As citizens rushed to carry goods to safety, a number of looters and thieves began running amuck. Others, hoping to cash in on insurance, set more fires. Firemen and police admitted to clubbing and shooting lawbreakers. One officer who stopped a would-be arsonist stated, "I do not know whether the man is dead, but I hit him hard enough to kill him. I stamped the fire out and let him lay where he fell." A Victor fireman told of catching a man cutting a fire hose and hitting him with a rock. The police ultimately announced that death would be dealt to all thieves and vandals.

The city's fire and police departments were hardly staffed for a fire of this magnitude. Special officers were sworn in to patrol streets and assure no more looting occurred. City officials had no choice but to recruit ordinary citizens to serve as "special police" to assist in the mayhem. The total number of men who suddenly found themselves deputized and forced into duty will probably never be known. Today, only a handful of treasurers notes issued by the city provide one of the only links to these men, whose honor and bravery indeed denotes them as "special." They received an average of $6.68 each for their efforts, but because the city coffers were in a bit of confusion, most were unable to cash their notes in for months after the fires.

Unlike the first fire, many people were caught by surprise by the second conflagration. More than a few met tragic ends before help could arrive. The actual number of deaths and injuries happened too fast to count or record accurately. Sisters of Mercy Hospital, two blocks below the reservoir, was saved

Businesses that escaped the flames of the April 25, 1896 fire considered themselves lucky. Even so, hundreds were left homeless as the city grappled with the disaster and struggled to clean up the mess. (Courtesy Cripple Creek District Museum.)

The El Paso Livery Stable was blown to smithereens in a vain attempt to stop the fire. Subsequent explosions, both planned and unplanned, injured people who were taken by surprise. (Courtesy Cripple Creek District Museum.)

by firefighters who surrounded the building and held off the flames. Inside, the hospital was filled with injured people. At least 16 were hurt as buildings were blown up on Bennett. As many as six others died trying to contain the fire or by sudden explosions from dynamite stored in unsafe areas. Registers from the hospital morgue contained items such as "Charles Griffith, head blown off" and "John Rose, arm broken and eye blown out." Several others escaped injury by sliding from rooftops ahead of the blasts and avoiding falling debris.

The fire eventually burned itself out, leaving approximately 400 buildings destroyed and a total of 5,000 people homeless in four days. As night fell, people scrambled for shelter. Again, some boarded trains to Florence and Colorado Springs. As word of the blaze reached Colorado Springs, Winfield Scott Stratton listened intently as fellow millionaire Jimmie Burns described the devastation to Colorado Springs Mayor J.C. Plumb over the telephone. Gathered with Plumb and Stratton were other notable figures, such as Spencer Penrose, Verner Z. Reed, and Irving Howbert. But it was Stratton who jumped on the urgency of the situation.

Stratton's background as a poorly miner had trained him to realize when people truly needed help. Now that he was a millionaire, here was a chance to help others who were less fortunate. Stories were already countless regarding his generosities, from providing bicycles to the washerwomen of Colorado Springs to purchasing

Cripple Creek's notorious fires of 1896 burned roughly one third of the town, including the entire business district. This view is looking north. (Courtesy Cripple Creek District Museum.)

homes for his key employees and donating trolley systems to the city. So it was not surprising that within 30 minutes of Jimmy Burns's phone call, Stratton had formed a relief committee like no other. Insisting that time would not allow for divvying up the cost and billing everything to himself, he lost no time in procuring a special two-car train to make the needed trip to Cripple Creek. Next, volunteers set to gathering a dizzying array of items from various merchants in Colorado Springs. Cases of canned beef, beans, condensed milk, and crackers were stacked into freight wagons and hauled to the Midland depot.

Colorado Springs' Colorado College canceled classes so students could solicit donations. Within hours, cases of food were gathered, including every available loaf of bread in Colorado Springs. Thousands of blankets and diapers were also collected, as well as 165 eight-person tents. With the goods loaded, the train pulled out for Cripple Creek at 5 p.m., stopping at various towns along the way to pick up more supplies. As the train made its way up Ute Pass, well-wishers ran alongside, tossing items to the workers on the cars.

In the meantime, Cripple Creek's fire victims had gathered at the city reservoir to find loved ones, figure out what to do, and keep warm by a scattering of campfires. At Gillette, the train whistle blew to let everyone know help was on the way. The sight of Stratton's relief train chugging into Cripple Creek at 9 p.m. that night must have brought tears to many an eye. It took most of the night to distribute supplies, which were handed out at the depot and loaded onto wagons for dispatch to the reservoir. Back in Colorado Springs, Stratton was organizing yet another relief train. The second train departed at 2 a.m. and arrived at dawn with everything from preserves and canned vegetables to liquor and cooking utensils.

Within three days, most of the homeless had rebuilt or found shelter and Cripple Creek was well on its way to standing once again on its own two feet. The mines of the district had remained closed so workers could help clear debris. The First National Bank of Cripple Creek opened in a charred warehouse to give pay advances. Supplies and money poured in from all over Colorado for several more weeks. The special police force stayed employed through May. Prominent citizens mixed with the poor to recover from the fires. As the garbage was hauled off and dumped in abandoned mine shafts, city authorities worked to reorganize and rebuild. The Cripple Creek City Council quickly wrote a new ordinance that even today stipulates that all new commercial buildings must be constructed of brick.

In hindsight, the citizens of Cripple Creek agreed the fires were actually a mixed blessing. Gone were the ramshackle wood frame structures thrown up haphazardly. In their places were beautiful brick structures comprising the "new" Cripple Creek. The new, fancier buildings attracted more newcomers and, within the next six months, the population increased by 10,000 people.

Between 1896 and 1899, both Cripple Creek and Victor were striving to become bigger and better. Their commercial businesses were strong, and the district consisted of several social classes from millionaires and business owners to miners and prostitutes. By 1897, Cripple Creek hardly looked as if it had been the victim of a devastating conflagration. All around the city, other district towns were flourishing as well. The F&CC began construction of a depot at Goldfield in 1897, and a year later the town had its street lights and telephone lines in place. Street car service was provided at 5¢ a ride. The Goldfield City Council hurried to keep up with Victor and Cripple Creek by declaring more ordinances. One ruled the speed limit at 6 miles per hour. Another disallowed loud or profane language in public. Goldfield was officially incorporated in 1899, possibly in order

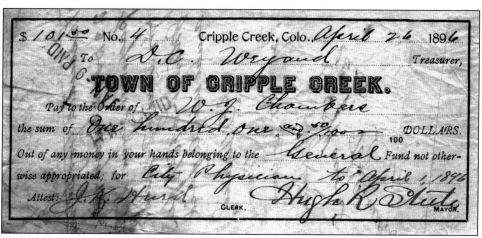

City physician W.J. Chambers of the Palace Pharmacy was lucky to receive his pay the day after the first conflagration.

to compete for the county seat. The ploy didn't work, however, and the honor went to Cripple Creek.

Still, within another year, Goldfield's population had risen to 3,000. District directories described Goldfield as a "lively little city" with seven boardinghouses, a variety of stores, nine groceries, five doctors, nine restaurants, and nine saloons. Clark's Opera House provided nightly entertainment. The F&CC and Midland Terminal railroads afforded transportation. In addition, Goldfield had as many as four schools and several lodges, including the Masons and Red Men.

When Goldfield was incorporated, the city appears to have taken the nearby town of Independence under its wing. Independence was located directly across the Vindicator Valley from Goldfield. Independence was originally platted as Hull City in 1894. Nearby was the Hull City Mine, a big producer through the early 1900s. Hull City was notable for at least one colorful character, A.G. "Smitty" Smith. A former Missouri farmer-turned-tramp, it is said Smitty had more tobacco stains than buttons on his shirt. Those tobacco stains must have

The city of Cripple Creek looked at its infamous fires as a chance to rebuild into a first-class city. By summer, several buildings were already up with more on the way. (Courtesy John Pitman Collection, Cripple Creek District Museum.)

been lucky; Smitty hit a rich vein and made $750,000 almost overnight. In time, Independence sprang up just below Hull City. The camp was named for Winfield Stratton's Independence Mine nearby. It wasn't long before Independence and Goldfield grew to meet in Montgomery Gulch.

Independence included up to 11 streets, including the main street of Montgomery Avenue. Its residents were working-class miners and, by 1896, the population reached 500. Businesses included an assayer and a jeweler. One boardinghouse and two hotels sheltered miners. There was also a drugstore, grocery, meat market, photographer, one physician, one restaurant, and two saloons. A lumber mill serviced mines, merchants, and homesteaders alike. The Midland Terminal dropped passengers off at First and Montgomery. Before long, a post office was established under the name of Macon for reasons unknown. In May of 1899, however, the name was changed to Independence.

Both Independence and Goldfield were considered suburbs of Victor, which had grown to become the second largest city in the district by 1899, right behind Cripple Creek. As early as 1896, Victor's population was already numbering 10,000. The city was connected to the rest of the district towns and mines via the narrow gauge Golden Circle Railway. In the wake of Cripple Creek's fire, the 1896 District Directory noted proudly that Victor's "fire department is especially efficient, being offered by men of long experience in eastern cities . . . the Victor Water Works adds greatly to the comforts and wants of her citizens." Despite this comforting fact, the city of Victor was unfortunately as vulnerable to fire as any western mining town. Fire struck in 1899 and the results were as devastating as Cripple Creek's fire three years before.

It had already been a busy year. In March, Victor had suffered another tragedy. A smallpox epidemic hit town, during which many children died. Fire Chief Frank Murray ordered the belongings of those families affected to be burned to prevent the disease from spreading. Mayor James Doyle ordered all churches, dance halls, and saloons to close. A quarantine was set up and, for several days, no one was allowed to enter or leave town. Another important event in March of 1899 affected the entire district with the formation of Teller County. When Colorado became a state in 1876, lawmakers established 17 original counties. In a time when the state was still largely rural with only a few thickly populated areas, 17 counties seemed adequate. With time, however, Colorado prospered into a tidy pot of gold with thousands of mining communities. The need to form additional counties was inevitable.

As early as 1892, gold discoveries in the Cripple Creek District were tempting residents there to form their own county. The county seat for El Paso County was in Colorado Springs, nearly 60 miles away, and revenues from the district often went to that city's coffers. Even El Paso County Commissioner J.C. Plumb agreed that as self-supporting as Cripple Creek was becoming, building all those extra roads to the district was costing more than the escalating value of that area. But Plumb and others changed their tune as the Cripple Creek District quickly boomed to one of the largest gold camps in the state and millions in gold was mined. The net taxable profits from all those mines meant a lot of revenue lost if a new county formed. So it was no surprise in 1897 when a bill for county division was voted down by the senate. Only 12 were in favor.

The defeat did little to deter residents of the Cripple Creek District from continuing their quest. Everyone from mine owners to miners knew there was much to be gained by forming a new county and continued fighting for division. For the next two years, Cripple Creek and other city governments pressed the issue while toying with what to name the county. The term Sylvanite was a candidate, but supporters of the division ultimately decided to name their new county Teller after Senator Henry M. Teller.

As the debate warmed, area newspapers commented at random on whether the bill would pass. The February 16, 1899 issue of the *Cripple Creek Morning Times* commented that the opposition from Colorado Springs was strong. In Cripple Creek, those for and against the division fought among themselves in traditional fashion. Many a bar fight broke out over the issue. In the end, however, the Colorado General Assembly passed the law and on March 13, 1899, Colorado Governor C.S. Thomas signed the measure to the officially create Teller County. Though small, the new county was nestled comfortably right in the middle of Park, Fremont, El Paso, and Douglas Counties.

To celebrate, Cripple Creek Mayor Charles Pierce declared a holiday and closed all schools and businesses. Only the saloons remained open as a grand parade made its way down Bennett Avenue. The parade was led by the chief of police riding a fine black mare. Mayor Pierce and Governor Thomas followed in a Victoria-style coach. The rest of the parade consisted of the fire department's new hook-and-ladder wagon, 6 bands, 2 drum corps, several floats, and 34 fraternal lodges. Float riders tossed Pear's Soap, Malt Nutrine, and Pozzoni's Face Powder to the crowd. A banquet at the National Hotel followed the parade, with a street dance held afterwards. Parts of the happy crowd dispersed into various saloons while various groups formed on the streets to carry on like giddy children.

Only one tragedy marred the celebrations when popular musician Joe Moore opted for a repeat performance by his Elk's Band from the parade earlier that day. Decked out in a purple uniform complete with brass buttons and gold fringe, Moore was leading his band back up Bennett Avenue just after dark. A group of spectators had formed behind the band, which wove its way across the sidewalks on either side of Bennett in a serpentine fashion. Along came Jim McVickers, who had been extricated from Lorimer's Saloon by Moore just a week before. Drunk then and drunk now, McVickers swore revenge on Moore. It came in the form of a single shot from McVickers's gun, which hit Moore in the head as he led his band. Within a few minutes, Moore was dead and McVickers was in custody. His trial was held in June, but the newspapers were vague as to whether he was convicted.

Moore's death aside, the *Colorado Springs Gazette* heralded the parade and several other celebrations as "a brilliant success" and cited many prominent figures, some from as far away as Denver, as participants in welcoming Teller County. In the aftermath, Teller County suffered the trials of any new county. Several laws were

Smoldering ruins awaited victims of the fire once the smoke cleared in Victor. Several weeks passed before the debris was entirely cleared away, dumped in nearby prospect holes, or hauled to the city dump. (Courtesy Cripple Creek District Museum.)

yet to be put in place. In the days when county laws were more stringent, it was also possible to avoid prosecution for breaking certain laws simply by stepping over the county line. Therefore, it is not so unusual that the Cripple Creek District saw an upswing in crime as lawmakers struggled to regain peace.

Thus, the city of Victor was already contending with these and other issues when fire consumed the town in August. In comparing the great fire of Victor to that of Cripple Creek in April of 1896, the incidents surrounding the fire are startlingly similar. Both fires began at about 1 p.m. In the resulting inferno, both towns also lost a good portion of their business districts. Finally, both conflagrations had their beginnings in the scorned and seedy part of town, originating in the red light district.

The Victor blaze began in a shack behind Rosa May's or Jennie Thompson's "999" dance hall, located near the corner of Paradise Alley between Third and Fourth Streets near Portland Avenue. Other sources say the fire began at the rear of the Dewey Dance Hall on South Third Street near Portland Avenue. Occupants of the shack were allegedly smoking opium, and either a lamp or gasoline stove was overturned. Quite before anyone had time to react, the flames had engulfed much of the red light district and spread quickly to the Monarch Grocery on the east corner of Third Street.

Unaware of the oncoming conflagration, two painters work away at the Gold Coin Club, lower right. Within a short time, the club with its new paint job would burn to the ground. (Courtesy Cripple Creek District Museum.)

Ironically, an article on fire safety had appeared in the *Cripple Creek Morning Times* just three months before. This handy piece included instructions on how to escape a building in case of fire: "If possible, never let a woman or child descend the rope alone. The husband should secure the rope under his wife's arms, place some article of furniture higher than the window, and then let the woman descend by playing out the rope gradually." How many people cut this article out and had it secured next to the kitchen stove? Furthermore, how many utilized the information while trying to escape the fire? It is more than likely that such advice was forgotten as folks scrambled to gather their belongings and escape to safety. Witnesses to the awe-striking blaze would recall that confusion, rather than common sense, reigned supreme.

Victorite Stephanie Hilliard recalled the story her grandfather Vic Moore told about the fire. The family was probably living on Fourth Street, at the time in the Irish section of town. Vic's mother, Lulu Ella Moore, was hurrying to pack up all the food, clothing, and other belongings she could. "All the women were trying to get those things they didn't want burned or blown up," Hilliard explained. To keep two-year-old Vic out of harm's way, Lulu placed him in an orange crate outside the home while she hurriedly packed. Vic later recalled seeing the flames creep towards them through the crate. "Even though he was little, he had nightmares about it for many years." said Hilliard.

Much like the fires of Cripple Creek just three years before, high winds spread the flames rapidly through Victor. The heat was intense enough to burn the fire hoses right out of firemen's hands. Horses and livestock ran wild. Goods were loaded into boxcars along the F&CC Railroad and rolled out to the siding, away from the fire. As with the Cripple Creek fires, looters ran amuck stealing goods, much of which burned anyway. When it became apparent that the fire was out of control, merchants and citizens acted quickly to construct temporary shelters for goods and families. Dynamite was used to blast buildings on the north side of town in hopes of saving the rest of the town. The Colorado Trading and Transfer Building of Victor was among those buildings blown to smithereens, thereby preventing the flames from spreading. Victor fire chief Frank Murray and Mayor W.J. Donelley quickly declared a state of emergency.

Later that night, J.A. Small, who worked for the Gold Coin Mine, would recount the scene in a letter to his wife who was visiting relatives in Maine:

> Well dear, to night there is practically no Victor: the Cripple Creek fire has been duplicated and since 1:20 when the fire started until 6 o'clock everything north of Portland Ave. has been burned. The area being bounded on the east by the Washington School and on the west by the Methodist Church, everything north of the two points mentioned is a mass of smouldering ruins and as I write, the big lumber piles north of the [Florence & Cripple Creek Railroad] are burning fiercely.
>
> I stayed with the office until the whole front was smoking and by that time the flames had enveloped the cribbing at the rear . . . We escaped through the ore house out on to the trestle, over the track . . . I thought best to take no chances and immediately started to put books, papers, etc. into the vault, which you know, is just completed. We filled it chuck full and got all the furniture out and by then the hotel was in flames.

The city of Cripple Creek was quick to return the help and support that had been offered by Victor three years before. Chief J. Knox Burton of the Cripple Creek Fire Department sent two companies to Victor when it was learned the flames were out of control. Cripple Creek's fire wagons were loaded into boxcars of the F&CC Railroad and chugged over as fast as they could. Even their additional help, however, failed to save the burning town. Victor's business section from First to Fifth Street and from Portland Avenue to Granite Avenue was destroyed. Included in the destruction were two railroad stations. The Gold Coin Mine's shaft house on Diamond Avenue and the Gold Coin Club, completed just a few months earlier, also went. "It was a tough sight to see the Gold Coin and our beautiful Club house go," Small noted, "and when the fire reached the boilers the old whistle commenced to blow and it sounded almost human in its wail . . . "

Incidentally, the Small home was guarded from the flames by a brick building occupied by the Victor Produce Company. Likewise, the Washington School was only badly scorched. But the Woods brothers, builders of the Gold Coin, lost a dozen properties. In all, 12 to 14 city blocks and 300 buildings were destroyed within two hours, with damage mounting to an estimated $2 million. Only the west end of the city was saved, thanks to a number of volunteer firemen. Nearly 3,000 people were left homeless. Injuries were numerous, including one Owen Lynch and four men who nearly died of smoke inhalation in a building at the corner of Second Street and Victor Avenue. Charles Wedig suffered severe injuries after being hit by a falling beam at the Colorado Trading and Transfer Company's warehouse. The number of thieves and looters resulted in the appointment of 50 special policemen.

By nightfall, several saloons and restaurants were open again. Many of the homeless had found shelter on nearby Battle Mountain, as well as in the generous homes of Cripple Creek. Hundreds of citizens set to work the following morning, clearing away the debris. By noon, Postmaster Frank Reardon had the post office back in operation. The *Victor Record*, which had managed to salvage its equipment, printed its newspaper as usual. A few days later, the Bank of Victor reopened, taking in one daily deposit of nearly $90,000.

As with the city of Cripple Creek, Victor looked upon the tragedy as a blessing in disguise. Property values shot up quite unexpectedly as would-be investors sought to buy burned out lots. Thousands of men set to work rebuilding. A myriad of finer, stronger brick buildings were started within five days to replace the rambling wood frames that had been Victor. Many of these buildings rose three and four stories high. "Tell Miss Fereman that the Gold Coin will keep on paying dividends just the same, without a break," Small concluded in his last letter to Ellie on August 28. "No one is discouraged and the contemplated places are much finer than the old ones."

Other entrepreneurs took advantage of the situation to make a bad thing good. Jennie V. Coyle, a bookkeeper and "copyest" in Cripple Creek, almost immediately set about publishing "A Souvenir of Victor Fire," which featured advertising from district businesses, as well as a full account of the blaze. The four-page pamphlet sold well and is a treasured collector's item today.

6. THE PEAK OF THE DISTRICT (1900–1904)

In the wake of Victor's fire, the Cripple Creek District quickly regained its balance and surged ahead, both economically and socially. The burning of Victor hardly affected other aspiring camps. One of these was Eclipse, which actually owed its existence to Victor. It is true that Eclipse was short lived and quickly forgotten; it was also one of the smallest towns in the district. For a small town with a short life, however, Eclipse was once an important facet in the district's growth.

When the Woods Brothers struck pay-dirt with their Gold Coin Mine in 1894, they took on contractor J.R. McKinnie. Despite the potential profits, having a monstrous mine smack dab in the middle of town posed a serious problem. Where to put the tailings? McKinnie solved the problem by drilling a tunnel through Squaw Mountain to transport and process the gold ore well outside the Victor city limits. The tunnel extended 3,700 feet through the mountain—no easy accomplishment in the 1890s. When it was finished in about 1899, the tunnel was alternately called the United Mine Tunnel and the Columbine-Victor Tunnel. The tunnel emptied out into what was later called Eclipse Gulch. Harry and Frank Woods financed the construction of a huge mill called the Economic Gold Extraction Company. In its time, the Economic gained notoriety as one of the first mills to use a chlorination process to refine gold in the district. Furnaces at the mill were fired by crude oil brought up on the F&CC.

McKinnie's plan worked well. At its peak, the Economic was processing 300 tons of ore daily and the Gold Coin yielded 30,000 tons of ore in one year. It was also probably McKinnie's idea to erect a small company town below the mill. Rather than shuttling back and forth to work, the Economic's employees could live comfortably just below the mill. Initially called Economic Junction, the tiny one-street town was finally called Eclipse, after the nearby Eclipse Mine. At Eclipse, business houses mingled comfortably with the suitably large homes built around and below the mill. The amenities were adequate enough for residents, who could trek a short distance up to the larger nearby town of Elkton if necessary. Victor was just on the other side of Squaw Mountain, and the communities of Barry, Mound City, and Anaconda were not far away.

If only for a short time, Eclipse became an important part of the transportation industry in the Cripple Creek District. Aside from the F&CC, the Midland Terminal Railway also serviced Eclipse. The Midland erected a railroad yard on one end of town and an aerial tram from the Cresson Mine ended at the yard. In addition, Eclipse reposed on the Cripple Creek District Railway's Electric Low Line. Eventually, Eclipse became known as a suburb of Elkton. Other nearby settlements included Arequa and Beacon Hill. The town of Eclipse appears only in the 1900 Cripple Creek District Directory, and it never had a post office or newspaper to call its own. Residents got their mail and telegraphs at Elkton. News came by way of the short-lived *Elkton Herald* or newspapers from Victor and Cripple Creek.

The year 1900 was an incredible year indeed. It was the prime of the boom and a time the district would never see again. The Cripple Creek Mining District produced $18,199,736 in gold that year, bringing the district's total production to $77,107,914. There were over 27 millionaires whose wealth originated in the district, and hundreds of prospect holes and mining endeavors dotted the landscape. The district's population had also peaked at 50,111, with 25,000 souls in Cripple Creek and 12,000 in Victor. The city of Victor alone boasted 20 groceries, 15 restaurants, 12 labor unions, 2 banks, 20 doctors, 15 attorneys, 48 saloons, 2 newspapers, and 6 churches. Even the *Denver Republican* reported, "Victor has risen to her glory from the piled char heap of late August like a blossoming rose bush."

The prominent Gold Coin Mine was the largest and wealthiest mine within Victor's city limits. (Courtesy Cripple Creek District Museum.)

Just behind Victor, Goldfield ranked as the third largest city with a population of 3,500. Elkton was next with 2,500 residents. Both Independence and Altman had 1,500 people, and Altman's school and city hall were doing just fine. Transportation in and out of town was provided by the Golden Circle and electric railways. The town employed a justice of the peace and had a volunteer fire department. Citizens could also frequent a number of organizations at Altman, including the Home Forum Benefit Order, the Ladies' Aid Society, and two chapters of the Red Men. A cigar store and four saloons also continued to service the town. Two unions prospered as well: the Free Coinage Miners' Union begun by Sam Altman and the Stationary Engineers' Union.

Anaconda's population in 1900 totaled exactly 1,059 residents, and the Anaconda Mine had evolved into a major producer. Anaconda's downtown consisted of two blocks of false-fronted buildings with hotels, saloons, stores, pharmacies, churches, and a white frame schoolhouse. Several doctors, lawyers, and even an optician called Anaconda home.

It is said Gillett's population peaked between 700 and 1,500 in 1900, depending on the source. Miss Mary A. Wilson was the principal at the Gillett School, which saw eight trains pass through daily. A new newspaper, the *Gillett Leader*, gave the *Forum* a run for its money for two years and the Co-Operative Brick Company supplied bricks for surrounding mines, homes, and businesses. Then, as suddenly as it had sprung up, Gillett began fading away. Both the Lincoln Mine and the

The Economic Tunnel solved major drainage problems in Victor's mines. Employees of the nearby Economic Mill were housed at the tiny community of Eclipse. (Courtesy Cripple Creek District Museum.)

King of Diamonds Mine played out and, by the end of 1900, Gillett was already losing its population.

Other towns of the district in 1900 included Beaver Park with a population of 75, Hoosier, Hull City, Portland Station, and Strong's Camp. Pisgah Junction, also known as Pisgah Park, was a suburb of Cripple Creek located at the base of Mt. Pisgah. Nearby but further west was Spring Creek, which was located roughly 1.5 miles north of Cripple Creek on the southern slope of Rhyolite Mountain. Spring Creek had its beginnings with several mining claims in the area. The tiny hamlet was located along its namesake creek in a pleasant and quiet valley.

Spring Creek was for all intents considered part of Cripple Creek, even though it was located nearly 2 miles from town. The town never had a post office, but if it had, Jacob Abby most likely would have been the postmaster there. Abby and his wife Josephine operated one of two dairies as well as a small farm at Spring Creek, along with Mr. and Mrs. Ed Neppel. Jacob Abby appears to have first come to Spring Creek in 1897 as the partial owner of several mining claims. By 1899, Abby had extensive dealings with several mines in the district, including the Hermosa Gold Mining Company. One of his business transactions involved Dr. William J. Chambers of the Palace Pharmacy in Cripple Creek. Chambers was the city physician and his wife Kitty has been the subject of much ghostly folklore at Cripple Creek's Palace Hotel.

Jake and Josie Abby were still living in Spring Creek in 1900, the only year that town appears in district directories. One source states 15 families lived at Spring Creek, but the directory sports a whopping 42 listings. There were few women. Among the men were Fred Desplaines, owner of the Union Dairy, and Charles Warner, owner of the Midway Dairy. Jacob Abby is listed as a carpenter. Spring Creek was also home to no less than 23 miners. Residents' children attended a little schoolhouse on the south slope of Copper Mountain, and Miss Alberta Smith of Cripple Creek taught classes there in 1900. In 1901, Abby sold an interest in the Little Lloyd lode to John H. Hobbs. The Abbys may have left Spring Creek as late as 1911; the 1920 census shows them as residents of Gillett.

Despite the family's departure, other people appear to have continued living at Spring Creek for at least a couple of decades. Of the few scattered buildings that represent what was Spring Creek, the cemetery is perhaps the most intriguing. Well hidden in the trees and located now on private property, the graveyard is said to contain as many as 16 graves. Two different sources state the cemetery was established in 1893 and that the Abbys' three children are buried there. It is said the children died of some contagious disease, but even old-timers disagree on what the illness was. Only one marble headstone remains to tell a sad, albeit interesting tale: that of Lloyd L. Abby, who died on January 25, 1896 at the age of five. The other two children were Clare "Nugget" Abby and baby Hazel Abby.

Lloyd was also memorialized in a mining claim that his father apparently named after him. Several other claims were located near the Little Lloyd: the Little Annie, Little Ellen, Little Emma, Little Jessie, and the Little Mary, any of whom may or may not have been Abby relatives. As for the true number of graves

Not much remains of Spring Creek today. The house in the foreground still stood as late as the 1980s. Two or three other buildings have met the same fate and have fallen to the ground.

in the Spring Creek cemetery, locals who spent time rambling around the area as teenagers recall seeing five or six wooden headstones. Some also remember an ornate wrought-iron fence that once surrounded the graveyard.

The cemetery is located at the crossroads of two roads that formerly led to Highway 67 and what is now the Bad Boys Turquoise Mine in Cripple Creek. It is the latter road that Jacob Abby and Ed Neppel likely took to sell their dairy products in town. Fresh eggs, milk, cheese, and butter were first-class commodities in the Cripple Creek District. From 1954 to the 1960s, there were still several cabins at Spring Creek. Most of them were dismantled or moved into Cripple Creek. One of them is thought to be located near Golden and B Streets. Back at Spring Creek, the few remaining buildings have silently fallen into decay.

Several other towns around the district appear exclusively in the 1900 district directory. The most prominent of these was Strattonville, a company town initiated by millionaire Winfield Scott Stratton. Throughout its short life, Strattonville was also known as Winfield, Stratton, and Strattonia. It was located along Range View Road, accessible from the Mollie Kathleen Mine above Cripple Creek or on the other side of the district via the town of Altman.

Strattonville was similar to other company mining towns across the state and even the nation. Neat rows of office buildings and homes were constructed at Stratton's expense to house miners and their families working at Stratton-owned mines. There was a clubhouse and one or two stores, plus a laundress on hand. But the similarities to other company towns ended there. The buildings at Strattonville were large and well-built. Unlike other company towns, such as the southern Colorado town of Ludlow that required their employees to patronize

Strattonville was the only successful company town in the district. Winfield Stratton's bedroom set from his town, as well as a pair of his boots and some spectacles, are now on display at the Cripple Creek District Museum. (Courtesy Cripple Creek District Museum.)

company stores with their over-inflated prices, residents of Strattonville were free to come and go as they pleased. Even Winfield Stratton himself kept a home on the property filled with beautiful furniture and the best in comforts. The only thing Strattonville may have lacked was a red light district.

Not far from Strattonville on Range View Road were three much smaller camps designed for the convenience of miners. The first of these was Vista Grande with a small itinerant population. Close by was Badger, a stop along the Golden Circle Electric Railway. The next stop on the railway was Midway, probably so named because it was located halfway between the Midland Terminal tracks above Cripple Creek and the town of Independence. The Midway Saloon, run by McKillip and Doyle, flourished for many years here. Sometime after the turn of the century, the libations at the Midway Saloon were accompanied by the services of French Blanche LaCoq, a prostitute whose face was burned with acid thanks to a jealous wife. In the south end of the district was Windy Point, located just half a mile south of Midway on the Colorado Springs and Cripple Creek District electric line. Many miners lived there.

The overflowing population of the district commanded every modern amenity imaginable. When the first automobile (an Oldsmobile) in the state was purchased by Canon City physician F.L. Bartlett in 1901, it was surely a sign of progress and things to come. The mere idea that one could take a drive in a carriage without horses was no doubt astonishing. The invention of the horseless carriage, combined with the fresh opportunities offered by a new century and a booming economy, likely made folks in the Cripple Creek District feel rather leisurely. Thus, when the town of Cameron was born, its primary goal to become the playground of the district fit right into the scheme of things.

It could be argued that Cameron was originally one of the first cities in the district. Back in 1892 during the battle between Fremont and Hayden Placer, Fremont founders Bennett and Myers had filed a plat on the northeastern most section of the former Broken Box Ranch and called it Cripple Creek. After Hayden Placer and Fremont combined to make the Cripple Creek known today, the first Cripple Creek remained empty until the Woods Investment Company from Victor purchased the land in 1899. During those years, the area was known as Gassy, as well as Gassey and Grassy. The latter name fit best, since Grassy was a series of large, grass filled meadows and rolling knolls. A small, rural population merited mention in the 1900 district directory. Both the Colorado Springs and Cripple Creek District Railway (CS&CCDR) and the Midland

McKillip & Doyle's Grand View Saloon was the only tavern at the junction known as Midway. The community housed only a few miners and their families. In 1906, Mrs. Prudie Breon of Midway is documented as having drowned in an abandoned mine there. (Courtesy Cripple Creek District Museum.)

Terminal Railroad skirted through the area. By 1900, Grassy was still known as a whistle stop on both railroads.

Taking advantage of the gold boom, the shrewd Woods Brothers founded the town of Cameron in close proximity to the Grassy site. The origin of Cameron's name is unknown, but it was a sure winner with two railroads chugging through it. In consideration of the devastating fires that destroyed Cripple Creek in 1896 and Victor in 1899, Cameron built its small commercial district of brick. The district ran the short length of Cameron Avenue and included three saloons. A newspaper, *The Golden Crescent*, was published for a short time at Cameron. Within a few months, the tiny town had a population of 700.

Cameron already had a Midland Terminal Depot, constructed back in 1894. An additional depot was constructed in 1901, this time for the CS&CCDR—also known as the Short Line. In its time, the Short Line became known for its pragmatic efficiency. The line extended to Colorado Springs, with ten tunnels adding to the excitement of the scenic ride. When Vice President Theodore Roosevelt took a ride on the Short Line in 1901, he expressed his satisfaction with the view by exclaiming, "This is the ride that bankrupts the English language!"

Allegedly, the Short Line also experienced celebrity status as the same railroad found on the board of Monopoly games. No expense was spared on the railroad cars, which sported ornate club cars and jaunty yellow boxcars. The Short Line also meant the birth of more railroad stops, such as Seward. This tiny community

The Colorado Springs & Cripple Creek District Railway was better known as the Short Line. Today, the scenic ride comprises much of Gold Camp Road from Colorado Springs to Victor. (Courtesy Kunkle Collection, Cripple Creek District Museum.)

had established a post office in 1896 and managed to survive to some degree until the Short Line came along. At that time, the name of Seward was changed to Clyde and the community even succeeded in establishing its own post office.

At Cameron, connecting trains veered off to Cripple Creek and Victor. Even the Midland Terminal could not compete with the Short Line. At one point, the two engaged in a fare war, during which round-trip tickets from Colorado Springs on the Short Line dropped as low as 25¢. The price was made even more tempting by the fact that Cameron was soon known as a resort town. Close by, the Woods Brothers built the playground of Pinnacle Park for the families of the Cripple Creek District. The park spanned 30 acres and cost $32,000 to create. The amenities of the day were there: a large wooden dance pavilion with a bandstand, a picnic area, restaurants, and an athletic field with seating for up to 1,000 spectators. Football and baseball games were the main attraction. Nearby, a zoo exhibited animals native to the area, including bears. There was also a children's playground, complete with swings and see-saws. Visitors could access Pinnacle Park by rail, horseback, carriage, and on foot. Even the occasional automobile made an appearance at the elaborate log-framed entrance.

Labor Day of 1900 appears to have been the record breaker for attendance at Pinnacle Park, when an astounding 9,000 people attended the day's festivities. Admission was 10¢ per head. The future of Cameron looked very bright indeed. Within a year, the nearby faded community of Touraine, which had a post office as early as 1889, moved its post office to Cameron. For a few more glorious years, thousands of visitors came to Pinnacle Park every weekend and holiday during the summer. But despite the park's popularity, Cameron's resident population never exceeded 700 people. This figure included the nearby suburb of Spinney Mills. Pinnacle Park's low admission price was exceeding the costs of running the park. Unable to make a profit at just 10¢ per head, Pinnacle Park eventually closed. Rumor spread that the Woods boys were in financial trouble. Lot sales at Cameron dwindled considerably, a sure sign of death in the gold boom era.

As Pinnacle Park floundered, an even more terrible event prophesied impending doom in the Cripple Creek District. On September 14, 1902, Winfield Scott Stratton passed away. Stratton's death signified doom in the district in more than one way. Almost immediately, human nature showed itself at its worst as an 11-year battle ensued over who got what of his estate. Though a noted reclusive alcoholic, Stratton's benevolence placed him far above his contemporaries. As time went on, however, Stratton became a sucker for a cause. In Colorado Springs, he donated the land for a new city hall and sold land for the post office to the government for half its value. Next, he built the Mining and Exchange building downtown. He also spent $2 million redeveloping the Colorado Springs & Interurban Railway. In addition, Stratton made generous donations to the Colorado School of Mines, Colorado College, and the Colorado School for the Deaf and the Blind.

Stratton's biggest concern was for the welfare of others. His employees received such Christmas bonuses as houses and tens of thousands in cash. It was said he

Although wealthy far beyond his needs, Winfield Scott Stratton's money deeply depressed him. His drinking habits and melancholy outlook aged him considerably before his death in 1902. (Courtesy Cripple Creek District Museum.)

even once purchased bicycles for every laundress of Colorado Springs. In the wake of his death, Stratton's good deeds were forgotten as a series of would-be widows and others squabbled over his estate. At risk were several mines in Cripple Creek, the Brown Palace Hotel in Denver, the International Realty Company, acres of real estate, and lots of cash. But his Myron Stratton Home, established to provide for the aged and orphans, was especially a target.

Named for Stratton's father, the Myron Stratton Home was finer than any other such home for indigents in the nation, if not the world. Expansive grounds included large children's dormitories and smaller private houses where the elderly could live out their days in comfort. At the Myron Stratton Home, Stratton's will stipulated that "the inmates of said home shall not be clothed and fed as paupers usually are at public expense, but they shall be decently and comfortably clothed and amply provided with good and wholesome food with the necessary medical attendance . . . " After several protests and thousands in court costs, the Myron Stratton Home was finally able to incorporate in 1909. Residents were admitted to the home starting in 1913. Even today, Stratton's money continues to finance the home, which still functions in essentially the same manner as it was originally intended.

Winfield Stratton's good deeds had included treating his mine employees fairly and encouraging other mine owners to do the same. With him out of the way, the mine owners, who had established the Cripple Creek Mine Owner's Association (CCMOA) in 1901, could now proceed to get the most bang for their buck out of employees. More towns and stations such as the Short Line railway stop of

Rosemont were continuing to sprout like weeds throughout the district. Over at Cameron, however, the population was visibly shrinking as the district launched into the second of two notorious labor wars. Cameron was located dangerously close to Altman and Bull Hill above Victor, where most of the action was taking place.

The eight-hour work day, which had become law in 1899, had been unceremoniously overruled by the Colorado Supreme Court. After three tries, the Western Federation of Miners (WFM) finally succeeded in its quest to restore the eight-hour work day in 1902. But money does funny things to a man's head, and most mine owners outright refused to obey the law. Then the WFM resumed rallying for support in Colorado City, where several mills processed Cripple Creek gold. News of strikes and the firing of union employees quickly made its way to the Cripple Creek District, where miners once more joined in demanding fewer hours, higher wages, and equal opportunity employment.

More union miners were fired. Lists of demands from the WFM were ignored. Within a short time, 1,750 Cripple Creek District miners walked off the job. Similar occurrences were taking place in Idaho Springs and Telluride, but the strikes at Cripple Creek were growing to violent proportions. Already, three union stores were in place to counter the CCMOA's refusal to extend credit to striking miners. By the end of August, skirmishes were taking place on a regular basis and Mayor Thomas French of Victor was requesting troops to be sent in. Throughout the district, memories of the strike of a decade ago came flooding back.

A mysterious fire at Altman in 1903 did little to quell the growing panic. In September, Governor James H. Peabody sent Brigadier General John Chase to investigate the goings on between miners and mine owners. Chase found everyone, including whole families and even businesses, pitted against each other. The Citizen's Alliance of Cripple Creek, numbering 400, was defending the mine owners and refusing to do business with union miners and their families. The whole district was on the verge of violence. Strikers and union leaders were being arrested, tried, and deported. On September 21, 22, and 23, armed guards surrounded the Teller County Courthouse as union leaders and striking miners were tried. Then, on September 29, the entire staff of the *Victor Record* was arrested after printing an unkind editorial about the mine owners.

Things reached an ugly peak when Harry Orchard, a professional assassin, was hired by the union to bomb the Vindicator Mine outside of Victor. The Vindicator was blown up on November 21, 1903, killing superintendent Charles McCormick and another man. Governor Peabody immediately declared martial law and the militia was brought in. The editor of the *Victor Herald* was told to keep his editorial comments out of the paper and a general vagrancy order warned that "Idle men will find employment or face deportation from the district."

Such deportations were outlawed by court order in January of 1904 and Governor Peabody revoked martial law in February. The state militia withdrew and the CCMOA jumped at the chance to root out and dispose of the union men. CCMOA cards were now required of all miners. Part of the application required giving one's background, listing a job history, and stating whether or not the miner was a member of the WFM. Racism also reared its ugly head and a good many rejected applications bore comments like, "This fellow is a Bohunk pure and simple and a black one at that" and "Traveling with Mexicans." Other rejections included notes such as, "When left office, went next door and inquired where union headquarters were located."

Partly due to this humiliating process, the state militia was called back in June when Harry Orchard next bombed the F&CC train depot at the town of Independence on behalf of the WFM. Thirteen men from the Findley Mine were killed and several more injured, and the district broke into total mayhem. The sheriff of Victor was forced to resign his office or be lynched. Following a mob fight in Victor, during which two more men died, the militia aided in arresting hundreds of miners, city marshals, and union sympathizers.

Adjutant General Sherman Bell of the state militia was in command of forces in the district and it was he who began issuing warrants, and threatening and arresting striking miners. Most of these arrests were highly illegal, rights and writs of habeas corpus being visibly absent. The arrested men were crowded into a bull pen outside of Victor, where blankets and food were scarce. Friends and families stood around the pen, giving what support they could while being held at bay by militia guns. Other sources imply that some prisoners were incarcerated and interrogated at the Elks Lodges in Victor or Cripple Creek.

Meanwhile, deporting procedures were set in place as 200 men were taken by train to various borders surrounding Colorado. Most were marched right up the main drags to the train depots and loaded into cars like cattle before departing for parts unknown. Many were beaten and robbed during the trip. At the border, orders to never return were emphasized with shots fired over the men's heads. Back in the district, a witch-hunt took place during which suspected union supporters were terrorized in their own homes. Most of the banished were taken in by the WFM at Denver.

In an effort to avoid deportation, a group of striking miners gathered at the F&CC Railroad stop of Dunnville, located just south of Nipple Mountain in Phantom Canyon. There, the group allegedly planned to attack and overtake the Victor Armory. The Pinkerton Detective Agency stepped in this time and sent guards to disperse the rebels, and a gun battle ensued. Amazingly, over 600 shots were fired with only one injury.

Back in the district, deportations continued through July when the governor ordered the military to withdraw and left things in the hands of the Citizen's Alliance. Accordingly, mob terrorist groups were formed, invading the homes of suspected union miners and dragging them off into the night before their terrified families. In August, a mob of roughly 1,500 men terrorized downtown Cripple Creek, wrecking a former union store and frightening citizens for several hours.

Later that year, the mine owners succeeded in electing their own men for the positions of county sheriff and district attorney. The WFM's terrorist acts, especially the blowing up of the Independence depot, had resulted in a drastic loss of supporters that could not be reversed. By the end of 1904, matters had settled down considerably and the mines got back to business. The El Paso drainage tunnel, a major accomplishment for water-logged district mines, was completed in 1904. At the time, it was the longest tunnel to be constructed in the district. By 1907, most cases against "union criminals" were dismissed and the union withdrew from the mines. The district's two notorious labor wars ended with one victory for each side.

In the midst of the fray, during November of 1904, a fourth great fire of the Cripple Creek District at Anaconda occurred and was practically forgotten. The fire originated at Nelson's Grocery Store at 11:30 p.m. and presumably had nothing to do with the strike. The ensuing inferno leveled most of the town and caused between $50,000 and $60,000 in damages. Due to low water pressure, there was little to be done. A few buildings were dynamited, including the city hall, but nearly every building in town was burned. Curiously, the newspapers reporting on the fire did not even make an effort to predict whether the town would be resurrected. Anaconda did struggle to rebuild, albeit half heartedly in the wake of the strikes and a general slow down throughout the district. Cameron also continued suffering a slow death as residents drifted off to other communities. The gold boom at what had been deemed "The World's Greatest Gold Camp" was coming to an end.

Harry Orchard's handiwork at the Florence & Cripple Creek depot in Independence killed 13 men. (Courtesy Cripple Creek District Museum.)

91

7. Characters and Famous Folk of the District

There is no question that, during its heyday, the term "Cripple Creek" was a household word across America and much of the world. To put it in perspective, the Cripple Creek District grew so large and famous that, two generations ago, everyone had heard of it and knew where it was. The Cripple Creek District fairly seethed with wealth and opportunity. Every modern amenity imaginable was available in this district, and its larger cities rivaled places like New York, Chicago, and Los Angeles in conveniences and lifestyles. And, like any brimming metropolis, the cities and towns of the Cripple Creek District sported a variety of people from all sorts of backgrounds.

Some of the transient population included visitors and residents who were, or eventually became, internationally famous. It is no surprise, therefore, that an overflowing handful of notable characters passed through or even called the district home. Some made their riches here; others gained their fortunes after leaving the district.

Lord William Lidderdale was one of many investors who took an interest in the Cripple Creek Gold Mining District. Formerly the governor of the Bank of England, Lidderdale was an important financial backer of the Colorado Midland Railroad. Lake George, a stop along the Colorado Midland Railroad, was originally named Lidderdale Reservoir. When the railroad reached 11-Mile Canyon outside of Lake George, the first stop was also called Lidderdale. Later, the governor was invited to Cripple Creek by Count James Pourtales, one of the earliest investors in the Broadmoor at Colorado Springs. Lidderdale arrived in the Cripple Creek District in 1891 to see about investing in some mining claims. History does not record whether or not he purchased anything.

Bob Ford was probably the first notable bad guy to make an appearance in Cripple Creek. Ford, who gained notoriety for killing outlaw Jesse James in 1882, was only 19 years old when he took his place in history. The story goes that on April 3, 1882, Jesse noticed a crooked picture on the wall and stepped upon a chair to straighten it at his Missouri home. Bob Ford, the gleam of a $10,000 reward in his eye, took advantage of Jesse's unguarded move. A single shot through the back

"That dirty little coward who shot Mr. Howard," Bob Ford was turned away from the golden gates of Cripple Creek. How history might be different had he been allowed into town! (Courtesy William Gibbons.)

of Jesse's head did him in. Next, Ford surrendered to local authorities, was tried, convicted, and pardoned immediately by Missouri Governor Thomas Crittenden. But the code of the West, which forbid shooting a man—any man—in the back, was less forgiving.

For several years following the killing, Bob Ford roamed the country. He was often denied a heroes' welcome, especially when he began touring and giving lectures on the incident. He was often booed from the stage and nearly lynched more than once. No doubt, Ford had trouble shaking his reputation as a yellow coward. Eventually, he landed in Colorado City, that wild and woolly place just west of Colorado Springs. But the unwelcome reception Ford received in other places was eventually echoed in Colorado City. In December of 1891, he was arrested for gambling. It was likely this incident that inspired him to seek greener pastures once more. This time, he decided to try his luck in Cripple Creek.

What Ford didn't know was that Cripple Creek authorities were very aware of his presence in Colorado City. Someone must have tipped them off about his plans to invade Cripple Creek, for Sheriff Hi Wilson met Ford at the city limits. Exactly what Wilson said to him is lost to history, but the conversation was enough to convince Ford that Cripple Creek wasn't his kind of place. On February 3, 1892, the *Colorado City Iris* announced Ford had gone to try his luck in Creede. Success came easier there and Ford soon found himself officiating prize fights and even running a dance hall and brothel out of a tent.

Ironically enough, Ford's newfound happiness was deterred briefly by a rumor that he had been killed in Creede shortly after he departed Colorado City. That fateful rumor would soon ring truer than anyone realized. In June, Ford was back at his dance hall tent in Creede. Ed O'Kelley was waiting for him. A former deputy sheriff from Pueblo, O'Kelley was one of hundreds who didn't like Ford. On June 8, according to most accounts, O'Kelley walked into Ford's, said "Hello, Bob!", and fired two sawed-off shotguns a mere 5 feet from Ford's throat. Creede went on to claim its own fame as the death place of Bob Ford and the answer to the question of what would have happened if Sheriff Wilson had let Bob into Cripple Creek will never be known.

Bob Ford's fateful departure from Cripple Creek was likely overshadowed by the arrival of Miss Lily Langtree, who, in 1892, performed at the Cripple Creek Opera House. A native of New Jersey, the "Jersey Lily," as she was called, captivated audiences for years. Her performances spanned from New York to Los Angeles, including hundreds of boom towns. Langtree is best remembered for her affiliation with the colorful Judge Roy Bean, a self-appointed sheriff and judge in Texas. Bean held a lifelong attraction to the colorful Langtree, even naming his bar the Jersey Lily.

Television's Dr. Quinn: Medicine Woman *was loosely based on the life of Dr. Susan Anderson, among others. Today, Doc Susie is the only known person at Cripple Creek's Mt. Pisgah Cemetery to have two tombstones—but only one grave. (Courtesy Cripple Creek District Museum.)*

If nothing else, Lily Langtree's independent lifestyle served as a role model to women such as Dr. H. Susan Anderson. Susan Anderson was born in 1870 in Indiana. When her parents divorced in 1875, Susan's father, William, took custody of Susan and her younger brother John. By the early 1880s, the family had moved to a farm near Wichita, Kansas. Living on a farm proved beneficial for Susan's later career as a physician. She learned to "doctor" the animals around the homestead. Susan's early knowledge of animal medicine, combined with her father's encouragement to pursue a career in the medical field, seemed to set her future in stone. But little did Susan realize her determination to become a physician would be challenged in several ways.

In 1890, William remarried to a woman named Minnie who appears to have been jealous of her new stepchildren. Far from being prepared for a ready-made family, Minnie already had two children and conceived at least two more by William. In her eyes, only her natural children counted as family. Minnie mistreated Susan and John at every turn. This abuse continued through the siblings' graduation from Wichita High School in 1890.

Two years later, the family moved to Barry, later known as Anaconda, in the Cripple Creek District, where William pursued mining interests. It was decided that Susan and John should attend college, serving two purposes: further education would broaden the teens' minds while simultaneously getting them out of Minnie's way. When Susan left to study medicine at the University of Michigan in 1893, Cripple Creek had eight physicians. By the following year, the figure had doubled. Susan planned to open shop in Cripple Creek upon graduation. But despite her good grades and aspirations, Susan received shattering news midway through her studies. Her father, influenced by the undermining Minnie, was cutting off financial support.

Undaunted, Susan borrowed money from a classmate to continue her studies. John also began working his way through school. With the relationship with her father at a standstill, Susan decided to find her mother. Marya Pile Anderson had remarried, but her heart was forever broken at William's sudden departure with the children. During their meeting, Susan learned her father had divorced Marya quite abruptly, with little explanation. Susan vowed to remain in touch with Marya the rest of her life. Susan's father was furious, insisting she cut ties with Marya, but Susan refused. When she graduated from medical school in 1897, none of her family attended. To complicate matters further, Susan also contracted tuberculosis during her internship. Still, she remained optimistic. A letter to her brother John revealed, "One of my instructors will be twelve miles from Cripple Creek this summer and I expect to see him sometimes perhaps."

Following graduation, Susan returned to Cripple Creek where she lived with her grandparents. Her relationship with her father was still strained. John was in California and Susan's friends were few. She set up shop in Suite #3 of the Bi-metallic Block (currently part of Womacks Casino). By then, 55 other physicians and 10 dentists were also calling Cripple Creek home. Being the only female physician in town must have been difficult. Her biography notes that Susan was concerned about the prostitutes from Myers Avenue who were infested with drug- and alcohol-related illnesses, venereal disease, and infections from back-alley abortions. Because of her unpopular status as a female doctor, it can be assumed that Susan's premier clientele consisted of many prostitutes.

Naturally, the pay was poor and she received no financial support from her father. In a letter to John, she wrote, "It makes me feel hard and bitter and sour when I have to go in old shabby clothes and scrimp and save and board off Grandma and Grandpa . . . " Meanwhile, Minnie and "her" children used William's money freely. Over the next three years, Susan worked at building her business.

Finally, one case established Susan's reputation as a trustworthy physician in Cripple Creek. A local boy had accidentally blown up some dynamite, breaking several bones. An attending surgeon wanted to amputate his arm, but Susan insisted on thoroughly cleaning and dressing the wound first. The boys' arm was saved and more people began coming to her. Within two years, she had repaid her college loans. The year 1900 looked very promising. John had returned to Anaconda where he worked as a miner at the Mary McKinney. Susan was residing next to her office at the Bi-metallic Block. Plans were underway for her to marry an unknown companion identified only as "W.R." in her diary.

Then, in a mysterious turn of events, William and W.R. had a falling out and Susan's fiancé broke off the engagement. On March 12, she sadly notes in her diary, "Pictures returned by W.R." In her misery, Susan hardly noticed the condition of John, who was living at Bolton House, a boarding house on Main Street in Anaconda. Just before Susan's prospective wedding, John had returned from a trip to California and caught the deadly influenza virus. By the time William and Minnie notified Susan of the severity of John's illness, he was delirious with pneumonia. On March 16, just a few days after the devastating end of Susan's pending marriage, John died at the tender age of 27. Susan's diary reads, "John buried today. He is gone from sight but is not far away . . . Life seems so useless and vain. No one now cares much whether I live or die. John was my best friend on earth and now my best friend is in heaven." Susan is the only surviving family member noted in John's newspaper obituary.

William Anderson, no doubt feeling guilty over his eldest son's death, moved Minnie and their children to California. Upon their departure, he issued a final callous command to Susan, forbidding her to stay in Cripple Creek. But Susan had already resolved to leave, traveling around Denver and working as a nurse in Greeley for seven years. She eventually moved to Fraser, located in Grand County, where she earned the nickname Doc Susie. She stayed in Grand County from 1909 to 1956, gaining her rightful reputation as a qualified medical doctor. Friends, associates, and clients all came to love her. Although her father visited her over the years, Minnie's absence is refreshingly noticeable in photographs marking the occasions. Perhaps William came to his senses and returned to the child he had come to mistreat in years past.

Dr. Susan Anderson died in Denver in 1960. She wanted to be buried next to her beloved brother John in Mt. Pisgah Cemetery, but the original family plot could not be located and Susan was buried elsewhere. Years later, the family plot was found. It is a grey marble pillar with the inscriptions of John, their grandfather, and a cousin on three of its four sides. Upon its discovery, Susan's inscription was finally added. Dr. H. Susan Anderson, M.D., has two distinctions in Cripple Creek: she was one of the city's first female physicians and she is the only resident of Mt. Pisgah Cemetery with two headstones.

On the more notorious front, at least two characters of the West also made an appearance in Cripple Creek. In about 1893, Wyatt Earp is said to have hung his hat in Cripple Creek for a short time. The events leading up to Earp's presence in Cripple Creek are well known: Wyatt met actress Josie Marcus after she surfaced in Tombstone, Arizona performing in the operetta *H.M.S. Pinafore*. In an instant, she stole him from prostitute Mattie Blaylock, who was allegedly his wife. In turn, Wyatt swept Josie out of the arms of Johnny Behan, who was destined to take part in the Earp brothers' infamous shootout at the O.K. Corral. Following that fateful day in October 1881, Wyatt beat a hasty retreat to Colorado.

In the spring of 1882, he retrieved Josie from San Francisco, where she had been sent in the aftermath of the shootout. The two traveled to Gunnison via Denver, but not before making a quick stop in Colorado Springs. One day, several local ladies were highly entertained by Josie, who was awaiting some companions at the Alamo Hotel in downtown Colorado Springs.

The women were shocked when three notorious gunfighters—Turkey Creek Jack Johnson, Sherman McMasters, and Texas Jack Vermillion—joined Josie. Before long, the group was accompanied by Wyatt and his brother Warren, who arrived on a Denver & Rio Grande train headed west. The group was in town

Wyatt Earp is purported to have spent time in the Cripple Creek District years after his infamous gunfight at Tombstone. (Courtesy William Gibbons.)

Bob Lee's arrest in Cripple Creek made front page news. J. Maurice Finn and two other attorneys represented Lee at his trial in Wyoming, but lost the case. Lee never returned to Cripple Creek, but Finn gained notoriety in 1901 as the builder of the Towers, better known as Finn's Folly. (Courtesy Wyoming State Archives.)

negotiating with Trinidad sheriff and friend Bat Masterson for the prison release of one Luke Short. Wyatt and Josie's stop-over near Ute Pass began a traveling stint that lasted for years. After Gunnison, the couple migrated to Idaho and later San Diego. In the early 1890s, the twosome left California and it is here that historians often lose their trail.

Two different sources say that Wyatt and his paramour next landed in Cripple Creek about 1893. Another source notes their residence as San Francisco at the home of Josie's mother. Josie herself recalled attending the World's Fair in Chicago that year. It is said they were in Cripple Creek for at least a year, but nobody really knows. The couple eventually settled permanently in Pasadena, California.

Shortly after the Earps departed the Cripple Creek District, or perhaps coincidental to their leaving, an even more notorious bunch decided to call the district home. Comprised of outlaws like Butch Cassidy, the Sundance Kid, and others, the Wild Bunch was well known in the West during the late 1800s. A lesser-known member, Bob Lee, was raised with Wild Bunch member Harvey Logan and his brothers. Logan, alias Kid Curry, was destined to form his own gang comprised of brothers Lonny and Johnny before becoming an integral part of the Wild Bunch.

The bunch managed to infiltrate Cripple Creek in about 1894. Wild Bunch associate John Lamb would later remember how the idea struck to send Bob Lee to Cripple Creek:

> Harry [Longbaugh, alias the Sundance Kid] says to me once, "Look, Bob gambles better than anything else. I've watched him. He's good. Why don't you set him up in a gambling house somewhere? Cripple Creek Colorado—that's a good place. We don't have any connections in Colorado. We might need a location down there someday."

Bob Lee, a natural winner at gambling, was soon offered a job running faro tables at the Board of Trade Saloon on Bennett Avenue. Lee balanced his time in Cripple Creek with bartending for his cousin Lonny in Harlem, Montana. Harvey Logan, under the alias Harve Wright, visited Bob Lee often along with other Wild Bunch members. Bob Lee later recalled meeting a man named Frank Scramble at the Board of Trade in 1897. Pinkerton's Detective Agency would later speculate that Frank Scramble was none other than the Sundance Kid.

In June of 1899, the Wild Bunch stopped the Union Pacific's Overland Flyer at Wilcox, Wyoming. The outlaws blew up a train car, sending $30,000 in bank notes fluttering into the air. This well-documented incident was immortalized in the 1969 movie *Butch Cassidy and the Sundance Kid*. The true participants in the robbery remained a mystery for sometime, but Lonny Logan and Bob Lee returned to Harlem shortly after the robbery and re-established their saloon business. Then, Lonny cashed in some stolen bank notes under Bob's name. The two escaped from Pinkerton agents by mere minutes and headed back to Cripple Creek. Wild Bunch associate Jim Thornhill later recalled Logan and Lee's escape from Harlem:

> One day Lonny comes steaming in on a lathered horse. "We got to hit the trail. George Ringwald paid me $300 cash and he'll bring $700 more to you soon. When you get it, Jimmer, send it in a package to Frank Miller, general delivery, Cripple Creek, Colorado. I'm going there with Bob. He's got a hangout in Cripple Creek."

There were three other Frank Millers in Cripple Creek, so Lonny's alias seemed legitimate enough. Lonny eventually received the money, said goodbye to Bob, and left for his Aunt Lee's house in Missouri where he was killed after Pinkerton agents surrounded the Lee home. The agents caught Aunt Lee burning letters from Bob, one of which was postmarked Cripple Creek.

The *Cripple Creek Morning Times-Citizen* had a full report on Bob's arrest on February 28:

> Robert Curry, alias Bob Lee, one of the most badly wanted criminals in the whole country, was captured in this city last evening and is now behind the bars of the county jail awaiting extradition by the authorities of Wyoming. Curry has been a fugitive from justice since June 2, when he and his two brothers, constituting the best part of a notorious gang, robbed a Union Pacific train at Wilcox, Wyoming and escaped to the hills with large treasure obtained from the express and mails . . .

Bob was dealing a game of stud poker at the Antlers Saloon when "The undersheriff walked straight up to him and asked if his name was Bob Lee. Curry looked up quickly and, with a suspicious gleam in his eyes, asked: 'What is it to you?' 'Well never mind,' replied Harrington [sic], 'you're the man I want. You are under arrest.' "

At Bob's trial in May, despite an aggressive defense by Cripple Creek attorney J. Maurice Finn, Lee was found guilty by his association with the Wilcox robbers. He was sentenced to ten years at the Wyoming State Penitentiary in Rawlins. Pinkerton agents went to Cripple Creek looking for Scramble and "the big Dutchman," as well as Harvey Logan. The search was fruitless. "We have not got the least thing," wrote Pinkerton agent Frank Murray, "not the slightest trace of the big German or any one up there who ever knew Frank Scramble and no one who seems to remember Harvey Logan."

Famous people of the district also included respected citizens. Born in what is now the Colorado ghost town of Rosita in 1887, Ralph Carr came with his family to Cripple Creek in 1894. Young Ralph grew up in the district, graduated from Cripple Creek High School in 1905, and went to work for the *Cripple Creek Times* in 1910. From 1912 to 1913, he managed the *Victor Daily Record*. Later, he attended law school at the University of Colorado and learned Spanish before migrating to Antonito and La Jara to offer free legal assistance to indigent Hispanic families.

From 1939 to 1943, Carr served as governor of Colorado. His chances at re-election suffered greatly when he refused to support Japanese concentration camps in America during World War II. "The loyal Japanese must not be made to suffer for the activities and hatreds of others," he told Americans during a radio address in February of 1942. "[They] are as loyal to American institutions as you and I."

Carr had already learned much about the Japanese culture from his stint at La Jara, where Japanese-American neighborhoods flourished. His close association with these people convinced Carr that the Japanese were not the evil tools of war Americans thought they were. At Colorado's best-known concentration camp, Camp Amache, Carr worked to make sure the "relocation center" was as comfortable as possible and even employed one internee as his personal housekeeper. The media in general hardly agreed with Carr's sentiments, however, and there was talk of impeachment.

After his stint as governor, Carr opted to run for the Senate. His opponents, however, seized the opportunity to attack his efforts at Camp Amache. In spite of the attacks, Carr managed to score nearly half the vote, losing to Edwin C. "Big Ed" Johnson. Even in his defeat, Carr remained humble by choosing not to reveal damaging information about his opponent during the election campaign. "I looked it over and felt that I didn't want to carry on the kind of campaign [Johnson] did," Carr once told his friend Frederick Lilley, "and so I left it unused."

Carr visited the Cripple Creek District one last time in 1949, accompanying Lowell Thomas and other notable celebrities on the last run of the Midland

Ralph Carr (middle) graduated from Cripple Creek High School in 1905. In 1939, Carr returned for an alumni prom just before being elected governor of Colorado. (Courtesy Cripple Creek District Museum.)

Terminal Railroad to Cripple Creek. In a series of interviews, Carr recalled his days with the *Times* and how he graduated from reporter to editor. He died the following year and today Denver's Sakura Square displays a bust of the former governor with a tribute to his humanitarian efforts.

Ralph Carr was just a child when William Jennings Bryan visited the Cripple Creek District. In 1896, Bryan was running against William McKinley in the presidential election in one of the most heated campaigns in history. One of Bryan's biggest supporters was Winfield Scott Stratton, even though Bryan's campaign included asking the government to start buying silver again. The plan would have devalued gold and cut Stratton's wealth considerably. Stratton later submitted a written letter to the press, explaining that he believed "free silver is the best thing for the working masses of this country."

The general public had little appreciation for Stratton's willingness to downsize his own fortune. Even more eccentric was Stratton's $100,000 bet that Byran would win the election. The wager stipulated that any takers had to put up $300,000 for McKinley. Stratton, already a multi-millionaire, planned to donate the winnings to the Colorado Springs Free Reading Room and Library Association. McKinley won, however, and Stratton handed over his money, probably glad to be rid of it.

Bryan visited Victor in 1899 on his campaign trail for the election of 1900. Once again, William McKinley won. A third nomination for president in 1908 also resulted in a loss. It was said that Bryan's visit to the gold district had something to do with ruining his political ambitions.

Another nationally known, if less famous, figure was Homer William Smith. A Denver native, Smith came to Cripple Creek in 1898 when he was only three years old. His father, a miner, was still struggling to recoup from the silver crash of 1893 when he brought his family of eight to town. As a child, Smith had a bad stutter and other speech impediments that left him behind in the social circles of school. He recalled haunting the district's abandoned mine shafts while satiating his constant desire to read. The stories of Mark Twain and other sophisticated boys' adventure tales intrigued him.

Smith also remembered vividly the labor strikes of 1904. "Violence was abhorrent to Cripple Creek, and the labor agitators, because of their use of it as much as because of the unfairness of the strike, were as popular as Carry Nation," he wrote in 1952. "To be identified with a union was to be branded as an anarchist, and from 1903 until I left town in 1910, Cripple Creek was a one-class town."

The Smith family emphasized education as one of the most important facets of life. Accordingly, Homer went on to get a college degree and serve on the faculty of New York University's School of Medicine. Smith authored a number of books, including his memories of growing up in Cripple Creek. More

Cripple Creek Bar Room *was actually filmed at Thomas Edison's Black Maria Studio in New Jersey. Notice the rather masculine barmaid on the right. (Courtesy Cripple Creek District Museum.)*

importantly to the world is his breakthrough study of the human kidney, which resulted in no less than three books alone. Smith died in 1962 and the American Society of Nephrology presents an annual Homer W. Smith Award to others who make outstanding contributions to kidney research.

Although he never actually visited here, one of Thomas Edison's first films was titled *Cripple Creek Bar Room*. The 45-second-long movie was actually shot in May of 1899 at Edison's Black Maria studio in New Jersey. It was, in effect, the first "Western" ever filmed. In 1904, the Selig-Polyscope Company's Colorado agent "Buck" Buckwalter filmed an 8-minute-long short called *Tracked by Bloodhounds; or a Lynching at Cripple Creek*. The scenes were shot on location during the month of April and included shots of Cripple Creek. Buckwalter was personally assisted on this production by Colonel William Selig, owner of the Selig Polyscope Company.

Even then, movie producers were willing to capitalize on sensationalism to sell their films. As it happened, the Cripple Creek District was suffering through the second of its two tumultuous labor wars. Buckwalter and Selig saw little action while filming in April. But when assassin Harry Orchard blew up the train depot and killed 13 men at the district town of Independence in June, Selig made the most of the premiere of his movie later that month. Advertising for *Tracked by Bloodhounds* insinuated that the events in the film were based on the real events taking place amidst the labor wars, and that the villain was actually a striking miner instead of the tramp that was portrayed. Newspapers across the nation, already aware of the explosion at Independence, further exploited the film in merely trying to get to the truth. Thus, the promotion of *Tracked by Bloodhounds* was some of the earliest media hype in United States history.

During the McKinley campaign in 1900, vice-presidential nominee Theodore Roosevelt was sent to the Cripple Creek District. Like Williams Jenning Bryan, his mission was to convince the voters of the district that producing silver coinage would be good for the economy and America as a whole. The people of the district, all of whom relied solely on the gold produced at Cripple Creek, weren't buying the story.

Despite three bodyguards that included Adjutant General Sherman Bell, Roosevelt's visit went downhill quickly. He barely survived making a speech at the Victor Armory before an angry mob of Bryan supporters began edging too close. The bodyguards, among them Cripple Creek postmaster Danny Sullivan, struggled to keep the crowd at bay and get Roosevelt back on the train.

In Cripple Creek, things went a lot smoother. Impressed by the scenery and gracious treatment by his hosts, Roosevelt promised to visit the district again in a few months. Attorney J. Maurice Finn offered to put Roosevelt up and the vice-presidential nominee accepted. In Roosevelt's absence, Finn borrowed tens of thousands of dollars to erect a palatial mansion in which to lodge the vice president. He called it the Towers.

Most unfortunately, time constraints did not allow Roosevelt to get any further than the front porch of the new home. When he had departed, residents around

Vice President Theodore Roosevelt returned to the district in 1901, where he visited the seventh level of the Portland Mine. He is identified as the man in the middle wearing the dark coat. To the left is Spencer Penrose. This photo was retouched for local publications. (Courtesy Roelofs Collection, Cripple Creek District Museum.)

the district renamed the Towers "Finn's Folly." Even Maurice Finn himself called it a "monument to a damned fool." The house eventually sold for back taxes and parts of it were used in another home in Denver. The rest of it was dismantled, and only ruins exist today.

Another honorable citizen to reside in the district was world traveler and radio personality Lowell Thomas. Lowell's parents, Harriet and Dr. Harry Thomas, moved to Victor in 1900 where Dr. Thomas opened his first practice. Eight-year-old Lowell grew up in Victor, attending the Garfield School while growing accustomed to the many bars and brothels Victor had to offer.

Lowell's parents, however, had much more lofty goals for their son. Young Lowell was taught the importance of a good education at an early age, emphasized by his father's impressive library of over 3,000 volumes on just about every subject. Both Dr. and Mrs. Thomas educated Lowell outside of his school time with lessons in reading, comprehension, and oration. When there was spare time, Lowell worked part-time jobs at a cattle ranch and several district mines, including the Portland Mine. Later, he recalled being a delivery boy for the *Victor*

Daily Record and the *Denver Post*. A few of his customers were ladies from Victor's red light district, who tipped him generously.

Other aspects of Victor also stuck in Thomas's mind. During the 1903 labor wars, during which Harry Orchard blew up the depot at Independence, Dr. Thomas was called upon in the middle of the night to help the injured. Lowell also remembered looking on with a cousin as a riot broke out at the Union Hall. Later, he was called to assist his father in moving an injured man to the doctor's office.

The Thomas family moved away for a short time in 1907, but returned to Victor within a year. In 1909, Lowell graduated from Victor High School and attended the University of Northern Indiana at Valpariso, where he earned a bachelor of science and master of arts degree. Upon returning to Victor, it wasn't long before Lowell's lengthy literary career began as a reporter for the *Victor Record*, the same newspaper he had delivered as a boy. Later, Thomas was hired as editor of the *Victor News* for $95 per month.

In 1912, Lowell returned to college with a scholarship to Denver University. He supplemented his income by reporting for both the *Rocky Mountain News* and the *Denver Times*, as well as working nights as a desk clerk in a Denver hotel. One of Lowell's first jobs after college was as a war correspondent during World War I,

Lowell Thomas traveled the world, but never forgot his beloved hometown of Victor. Here, Thomas is flanked at a 1967 reunion by two other well-known characters of Cripple Creek, author Mabel Barbee Lee and Rufus Porter, a.k.a. the Hardrock Poet. (Courtesy Cripple Creek District Museum.)

during which he actually donned some skis in order to follow and interview the Italian forces. He also married a fellow college student, Fran Ryan. In the years to come, Fran would often accompany Lowell on his many excursions.

As an explorer, foreign correspondent, lecturer, and writer, Lowell began recording his adventures and eventually turned his travelogues into a successful radio and television broadcast career. In addition, he published 52 books about his adventures. As a radio announcer, Thomas became known for his familiar opening and closing, "Good evening everybody," and "So long until tomorrow." All told, Lowell Thomas spent 46 years in radio and became associated with such notables as T.E. Lawrence, whom he accompanied through the Arabian desert by horseback and even on camel. Thomas's book *Lawrence of Arabia* was one of his many bestsellers. Other adventures led Thomas to Afghanistan, Alaska, India, and Tibet.

But he never forgot his beloved Victor, and he visited often. Frequently, he was the honored guest at parties and occasionally broadcast his radio show from the district. When he retired in 1976, Thomas informed the public of his plans via radio from Victor. He died in 1981, just two weeks after his last visit to town during which he talked of his life on film. Today, the Lowell Thomas Travel Journalism Award is an annual competition for writers striving to follow in his footsteps.

While several prominent men passed through the Cripple Creek District, none of them left quite an impression as a young lady named Texas Guinan. In about 1902, Texas and her mother were visiting Mrs. Guinan's sister Mrs. Margaret Conley in the district town of Anaconda. Mrs. Guinan's sister and her husband William lived just east of the Midland Terminal Railroad tracks. Theirs was a simple life; William was a miner at the Mary McKinney Mine. The family lived on Main Street and were devout Catholics who appreciated their comely status. When Tex and her mother showed up, they seemingly fell right in with the Conleys. It is said that Texas made her way in Anaconda by playing the organ for the Sunday school there.

But differences between Mrs. Guinan and her sister soon became apparent. When Mrs. Guinan began dressing Tex in rather garish clothing and making her face up with rouge and lipstick, eyebrows were raised. Those eyebrows raised even more when various men began traipsing after Tex, seeking her affections. If the townsfolk of Anaconda found Texas's dress and ways alarming, they were just as puzzled by her mother's actions. For wherever Tex went and with whom, her mother tagged along with a watchful eye.

Although Mrs. Guinan may have chaperoned her daughter's numerous dates, she does not appear to have interfered with the treatment of Texas's suitors. In fact, Tex gained quite a reputation for casting off men as frequently as she changed her high fashion wardrobe. Those who voiced their objection at being dumped by Texas were given a standard reply by the woman in question: "Oh, you poor sucker." Walter "Tug" Lee, a barber who worked just a block away from the Conley's home in Anaconda, served many a crestfallen admirer of Texas Guinan. Lee would jokingly greet these men with a sympathetic, "Hello, sucker!"

Texas Guinan rose from Sunday school organist to speakeasy queen and actress. One of her husbands, Johnny Moynahan, not only had a street named for him, but also platted his own addition to Cripple Creek. (Courtesy Leland Feitz Collection, Cripple Creek District Museum.)

In 1904, Texas finally met her match in Johnny Moynahan. A Denver newspaper artist, Moynahan had been investing in Cripple Creek real estate since the early days. His projects included establishing a housing project and the now defunct Moynahan Street (sometimes misspelled Mognahan) was named for him. Tex married him on December 2, 1904, but the marriage ended two years later.

Tex carried her trademark slogan with her after she left the Cripple Creek District. She used her charms to make her way to New York, where she ran a series of successful nightclubs and dabbled in movies and productions. In the early days, she performed in a number of amateur theater productions, most of them Wild West dramas. One of her first appearances in film occurred in 1913, when she was in the cast of *Hop O' My Thumb*, starring DeWolf Hopper. By the 1920s, Tex was a colorful divorcée who was running one of several speakeasies in Manhattan. Throughout Prohibition, Texas was able to run a number of successful clubs in a variety of locations. Two of them were known as El Fey and the Culture Club.

At Tex Guinan's, the party began at 11 p.m. and often lasted through the wee hours of the morning. Tex reigned supreme, greeting her patrons with her signature "Hello, Suckers!" and encouraging them to "Leave your wallets on the bar!" Each time she was raided and shut down, Tex simply moved to a new location and opened for business once more.

Throughout her career, Tex continued to dabble in film, earning a part in *Padlock* in 1927. By 1928, she had gained much notoriety. Eventually, she moved to Hollywood, where she ran with the likes of Clare Booth Luce, Dorothy Parker, Florence Ziegfield, and Clara Bow. Her connections got her back into acting and she appeared in the 1933 Broadway production of *Through A Keyhole*. Later, she ran a series of boardinghouses for rising starlets, organizing discreet gatherings out of the public eye.

When Texas Guinan finally faded from sight, she made a quiet and graceful exit. Her name is lightly mentioned in bits and pieces of others' memoirs. During a trip to Canada in 1933, she died of a stomach ailment. Three films have immortalized her since: *Lady for a Day* (1933); *Incendiary Blonde* (1945); and *Splendor in the Grass* (1961). Were Texas here today, she might provide more insight to her colorful life. Of course, she'd likely leave out the fact she got her beginnings in the church at Anaconda.

Another celebrity of note was Julius Marx, better known as Groucho. In 1895, five-year-old Julius began singing at the urging of his Aunt Hannah. Little did he know that his performances were the ticket to his career at the time. The year 1903 found Julius leaving the seventh grade—and school—forever. His mother

In spite of his harrowing experiences in the Cripple Creek District, Groucho Marx did sign a photo for his fans years later. (Courtesy Cripple Creek District Museum.)

thought, as they did in those times, that Julius was better off supplementing the family income than learning things he probably would never use. Accordingly, Julius's first job was scrubbing wigs with kerosene at Hepner's Wig Factory in the theatrical district of New York. In the summer of 1905, he answered an ad in the *New York Morning World* newspaper that seemed tailored for him: "Boy Singer wanted for Touring Vaudeville Act. Apply Leroy, 816 3rd Ave., between 2 and 4."

Gene Leroy hired Julius at $4, as well as Johnny Morris, or Morton, or Kramer—whichever version of Julius's story one cares to believe. In any case, Johnny tap danced while Gene and Julius sang. The Leroy Trio was formed; Julius was barely 15 years old. The threesome set out for their first show at the Ramona Amusement Parlor in Grand Rapids, Michigan, followed by a performance scheduled at the New Novelty Theater in Denver.

Julius would later remember how Leroy and Johnny mistreated him throughout the trip. And although he didn't know it at the time, he later deduced they were homosexual. To make matters worse, the opening night of the show didn't go well. Johnny's shoe flew off in the middle of the performance and sailed into the audience. The venue only paid $60, but the manager fined the act $25 for the shoe incident. The misbegotten trio left town in anticipation of a better show in Denver. Julius was apparently unaware of the show's circuit beyond Denver. "From there," he remembered, "we went to Colorado to some town where there was an Elk's Convention. All the Elks were drunk."

Next, the trio traveled south. By chance or because they couldn't book a show, the Leroy Trio bypassed Colorado Springs and ended up in Cripple Creek. The details of exactly what happened next are sketchy. What is known is that Julius woke up one morning to find that Leroy and Morris had left town. The final insult came when Julius discovered the $8 he had saved up in a chamois sack under his pillow was gone, too. With the show folded and his money gone, Julius was forced to get a job driving a grocery wagon between Cripple Creek and Victor. "I didn't know anything about horses except they ate sugar," he later recalled. "The only horses I had seen up to that time were either on carousels or the broken down ones that pulled wagons on the streets of New York."

With his limited experience, Julius was no match for a gold camp district. "I was terrified," he would later confess, "because I had to go over this mountain and when I looked down . . . Christ, there must have been a 4,000-foot drop!"

Indeed, to a city boy at 10,000 feet above sea level, every valley and cliff must have looked perilous. "If I went faster it would be over sooner, I thought. However, one of the horses went on a sit-down strike in the middle of the road." The horse refused to budge until a new driver came along. In his biographies, Julius later claimed the horse actually dropped dead. The truth has been lost to history.

Whatever the real story was, Julius next went to work at a store that had been converted into a movie theater. "I would sing to various slides which would be projected on the screen." But the wild atmosphere of Cripple Creek theater proved to be too much and Julius eventually wired his mother in New York. Upon hearing of her son's desperate circumstances, Minnie sent him money to come back home. In time, he teamed up with his brothers to form a comedy act that is still some of the most popular wisecracking slapstick the world has ever seen. The boys from New York christened themselves the Marx Brothers, led by their infamous sibling Julius—better known as Groucho.

Carrie Nation, that notorious saloon-smasher of the Victorian era, visited Cripple Creek in 1906. Devout in her mission, the axe-wielding Nation was already well known across the country. On several occasions, Carrie had marched into many a saloon and calmly announced, "I am going to smash this place up," before proceeding to do so. "I smashed five saloons with rocks," she once claimed, adding "God was certainly standing by me."

Two stories surround Carrie Nation's visit to Cripple Creek. In one version, she never gained entrance to the taverns of Cripple Creek and had to settle for giving a fire-and-brimstone sermon in front of Johnny Nolon's Saloon. In the more racy version, Carrie allegedly trounced into Nolon's. Spying some obscene painting above the bar, she proceeded to smash her way right into the arms of the law, who put her in jail for the night. The next morning, Johnny Nolon himself was said to have bought her one-way train ticket out of town. Suspiciously, the latter story strongly resembles Carrie's first saloon-smashing of note, which actually happened in Wichita, Kansas.

It is known for certain that Carrie passed out miniature hatchet lapel pins, some complete with a jewel in the blade. She most certainly lectured to whomever would listen, including crowds at the Odd Fellows Hall and the Salvation Army. Homer Smith later recalled watching Carrie smash some saloon windows. Beyond that, the true extent of the havoc she wreaked is lost to history.

The fame of Carrie Nation ranks right up there with boxer Jack Dempsey, who worked at the Portland Mine while training for his boxing career. Born in Manassa, Colorado, Dempsey got his start under the name Kid Blackie in the Cripple Creek District. The Dempseys may have been in the district as early as 1900. A Mr. and Mrs. John Dempsey ran Dempsey's Exchange in Goldfield. M.F. Dempsey was a Victor miner, and there was another unnamed Dempsey listed at Irene and Third in Cripple Creek. It is also said that Jack ran a bar in Colorado City, west of Colorado Springs.

One story about the start of Dempsey's career centers around his alleged brother John, who first appears as a miner in Cripple Creek in 1902. Another source states that Jack's brother was Bern Dempsey. Sometime between 1907 and 1913, Jack arrived from Telluride to work alongside his brother in the mines. His first job was at the Mollie Kathleen, although he might have worked at the Portland as well. Bern was working at the Golden Cycle Mine. At one point, the brothers leased a mine together, but it played out.

In his off time, Jack trained on the second floor of Victor City Hall and boxed at the Gold Coin Club in Victor. One of his first fights was in December of 1907, when the *Cripple Creek Times* reported that Kid "Blacky" would be fighting J.W. "Kid" Thomas on Christmas Night in Victor. Some historians say the most exciting fight of his career took place in 1913 against George Coplen at the Lyric

Opera House in Cripple Creek. Coplen had been in the district since 1893, beginning with his career as a miner in Mound City. Dempsey won the fight against Coplen in the seventh round. Dempsey went on to win several more heavyweight titles and gain world fame.

Jack Dempsey fought his last fight in 1927, just about the time that future art critic Robert Coates was getting ready to leave his childhood home in Victor and see the world. Coates later worked for *The New Yorker* magazine during the 1940s. In the art critic world, Coates is best known for coining the phrase "abstract expressionism."

Jack Dempsey, the Manassa Mauler, had his humble beginnings in the makeshift boxing rings of Victor. This rendition of his famous stance hangs at the Cripple Creek District Museum alongside a pair of his boxing gloves. (Courtesy Cripple Creek District Museum.)

8. SLOWING DOWN (1905–1914)

By 1905, the cases against the WFM during the Cripple Creek District's second notorious labor war had been dropped. The Cripple Creek District fell into ease as memories of the violence the year before slowly faded. Only cases such as the 1906 trial of James Warford remained as the last testament to the bloody and violent strikes. During the labor strikes, Warford had killed Goldfield constables Isaac Leibo and Chris Miller, who refused orders to "move along." Warford claimed self defense and eventually was freed.

Furthermore, mining production was slowly spiraling downward. Mining was getting expensive. Roughly 10 percent of the district's mines were over 1,000 feet deep and many of them were beginning to fill with water from deep underground streams. In answer, construction began on the Roosevelt Deep Drainage Tunnel in 1907 to help alleviate the problems. Social changes were also coming. In Victor, Augusta Reardon was elected the first female postmistress. But suffragettes like Augusta were still being undermined by such women of the underworld as Lizzie Stevenson and Neoma Hodge. The newspapers reported on both women in 1907. Stevenson was arrested and fined $1 for being in a "beastly state of intoxication," and Hodge and her husband Dave were arrested after a stray shot from Hodge's pistol hit Dave in the head.

Indeed, crime both past and present was leaving its mark within the district. The incidents ranged from tame, such as the November turning loose of five Thanksgiving turkeys in Goldfield, to the gruesome discovery of body parts in the walls of Cripple Creek's old Pikes Peak Hospital during its demolition later that month. Still, the communities of the district were heartened by the official ending of the 1903 strikes by the executive board of the WFM.

At Christmas, Santa Claus appeared at the Boston Department Store in Cripple Creek and the Salvation Army delivered 24 Christmas boxes in Cripple Creek and two in Anaconda. The good charity was extended to nearly everyone, it seemed. The Vindicator Mine gave their employees $5 gold pieces for Christmas and Victor Post Office employees each receive a box of cigars. Those wishing to vacation for the holiday could take a round trip on the CS&CCDR for $2.75 to

Construction began on the Roosevelt Drainage Tunnel in 1907. When completed, the tunnel provided much-needed drainage from district mines. (Courtesy Cripple Creek District Museum.)

Colorado Springs, $4.10 to Pueblo, or $5 to Denver. But the big treat came in a Christmas night boxing match in Victor. The contenders were "Kid Blackie," later known as Jack Dempsey, and J.W. "Kid" Thomas. Elsewhere in Victor, the Victor Opera House presented *The Mayor of Tokio*, *Buster Brown*, and *The Showgirls*. During the course of the festivities, no less than ten intoxicated men were jailed for fighting in Cripple Creek.

Such merriment barely masked the fact that the district was still slowing down. In January of 1908, A.E. "Bert" Carlton took over the work on the Roosevelt Tunnel, which was experiencing financial difficulties. Unexpected hard rock had resulted in much slower progress and the project was costing twice as much to build. The district mines could expect to be fully underwater in just a few years, said Carlton at a meeting of mine owners, unless the tunnel was finished. Back in 1899, Carlton had sold the Trading and Transfer Company to the Midland Terminal Railroad, vacated the modest apartment on the top floor of the building, and moved into the more spacious suites atop his First National Bank. As Cripple Creek's economy slowly declined, Carlton was known to invest his wealth back into failing properties, including those he had sold, in an effort to save them.

Unfortunately, Carlton's benevolent acts could not save the district. The post offices at Anaconda, Cameron, and Clyde each closed in 1909. The district also lost two of its most notable characters with the deaths of gold discoverer Bob Womack and Cripple Creek's first madam, Blanche Burton. Carlton's Roosevelt Tunnel was completed in 1910, but the point nearly seemed moot. By then, the

113

Albert Eugene "Bert" Carlton did much to assist the ailing Cripple Creek District when the mines began giving out. (Courtesy Cripple Creek District Museum.)

stagecoaches of Shelf Road were being replaced by motor coaches, even though most of them had to be backed up the steep hills in order to get the maximum power. Times were changing. Despite the decline, however, Bert Carlton was undaunted. Bert and his wife Ethel established the Golden Cycle Corporation in about 1910. Over the next 50 years, Golden Cycle would become one of the largest mining conglomerates in the district, acquiring nearly all but about a quarter of the active mines in the district. The Carltons also financed a variety of other businesses throughout Colorado, including Holly Sugar Corporation.

If the Carlton's benevolent investments proved successful for Bert and Ethel, they did not do so much for the Cripple Creek District. Water in the mine shafts was still a problem, but gold was also becoming too expensive to mine. Whole towns were abandoned as people moved on to greener pastures. Other families chose to stay on, turning to other ways to make a living. But throughout 1911 and 1912, the district continued to flounder. The Anaconda post office was re-established in 1911, but the post office at Altman was discontinued.

Then, the body of James Warford, the deputy sheriff who was tried in 1906 for the murders of two Goldfield constables, was found beaten and bullet riddled on Battle Mountain in 1912. His killer was never found. Things took an even uglier turn when a 30-foot wall of water destroyed 5 miles of track on the F&CC. The track was never rebuilt. There was, however, a new light at the end of the tunnel. In 1912, a summer issue of the *Cripple Creek Times* reported 1,700 visitors to the district on one day. It was the first time evidence surfaced that the district could potentially evolve into a tourist resort.

With mining losing its prominence in the daily news, local papers scrambled for something to talk about. Important business news was replaced with such stories as the one about John Nixon, who was arrested for abusing a turkey on Cripple Creek's Bennett Avenue. In the end, the bird squawked so much that the arresting officer beheaded it with an ax and let Nixon go. Other Thanksgiving happenings included a ball held at the Union Hall in Cripple Creek and a sale at Simmons Grocery for turkeys at 26¢ per pound.

But the district, bored with such bland accounts, yearned for something juicier. Readers of the *Cripple Creek Times* and the *Victor Record* eagerly read about a 1913 gambling bust in Victor and attempted roller skating, the latest craze. They debated over whether B.J. Medill's store and the Three Rules Store of Cripple Creek were right to shorten their female employee's workdays to eight hours. They gasped when Pikes Peak was found to be 1 foot higher than originally thought. And they frolicked in the snow when a severe storm dumped over 9 feet in December.

On the mining front, the industry continued to sink. Gillett's post office closed due to the slump and Winfield Stratton's company town, Strattonville, was officially declared a ghost. Many mines began opting for the "split check" system between leasers and lessees. Essentially, individual miners could lease mines from their owners for a portion of the profits, usually 50/50. Leasing arrangements were

Gillett, nearly a ghost town since 1905, was among the first district towns to die. This is Father Volpe's Catholic Church, fast on its way to becoming a hay barn. (Courtesy Cripple Creek District Museum.)

a viable way to keep the mines open. No money was required up front and leasing to an individual was less costly than the overhead necessary to operate an entire corporation. As time went on, the lessees were sometimes comprised of a group of partners. No amount of incorporation, however, could prevent the constant dangers of working in a mine. In 1913, a cave-in at the Golden Cycle Mine killed five men. But a reprieve was just around the corner. In 1914, Cresson Mine manager Richard Roelofs hit one of the last great strikes in the district.

The Cresson had originally sunk its first shaft in 1894. The name of its original owner is unclear, but history states that J.R. and Eugene Harbeck of Chicago were the owners who matter most in this tale. Allegedly, the two awoke from a night of partaking in potables to find themselves owners of the Cresson. Possession of the mine was no notable feat. It was located about a mile above the town of Elkton in rough terrain and was worthless to boot.

To complicate matters, the brothers Harbeck had no money to develop their mine. Instead, they relied on good news about the district to attract investors back home. Occasionally, they were able to sell a little stock, which was invested in the profitless hole on the mountain. The mine was also occasionally financed by leasing various parcels to prospectors. Frank Ish, former owner of the *Cripple Creek Crusher* newspaper, sank a 600-foot shaft at the Cresson and found nothing.

While the Cresson failed, the area around it flourished. In 1905, the population of Elkton reached 3,000, comprised mostly of miners who worked in the surrounding hills. Charles Waldron had been managing the Cresson. When he gave up, the Harbecks hired Richard Roelofs, a civil engineer with little mining

Richard Roelofs (middle, with white hat band) looks quite at home amongst the miners in this early photo. (Courtesy Cripple Creek District Museum.)

experience. Roelofs reluctantly began working the 600-foot shaft left by Frank Ish. Three years later, Roelofs was still plugging away with several useful inventions under his belt; one was a safety trip used to make running the cage out of the shaft safer. He also erected an ariel tram to run down the hill to Elkton. Most importantly, Roelofs was pulling low-grade ore from the Cresson which assayed at $15 to the ton. It wasn't much, but it was better than most mines were producing.

Roelofs kept at it. By 1910, rumor was that "the miracle miner" had extracted $60,000 in gold from the Cresson. During the following year, the mine rose out of debt. By 1913, the Cresson was earning $150,000 in annual profits. Folks of the district suspected the figures to be mere speculation mixed with wishful thinking until November 1914, when Roelofs urgently summoned Hildreth Frost, the mine's bookkeeper in Colorado Springs, to Cripple Creek. Upon arriving in Cripple Creek, the accountant made his way to where Roelofs was lodging at the Palace Block.

The following morning, Roelofs was escorted at his own insistence by Frost and another mining pioneer, Ed De LaVergne, to the Cresson. The three men descended into the depths of the mine. At the twelfth level, De LaVergne and Frost saw what Roelofs was so excited about. Within the mountain was a cavern, called a "vug" in the industry. The cave was 40 feet high, 23 feet long, and 13.5 feet wide, and the walls covered with oxidized gold flakes nearly an inch in diameter. Gold was literally flaking off the walls. The giant geode was worth a fortune. The discovery gave Cripple Creek a brief reprieve from its destiny as a dying mining district. In the first week, miners literally scraped the gold by hand from the walls. Nearly $40,000 of gold was taken. Within a month, the vug produced 1,400 sacks and $1.2 million worth of gold at $20.67 per ounce. At today's prices, this gold would be worth over $20 million.

Robbery, of course, was a primary fear. Heavy vault doors were installed at the mine entrance and miners were required to change their clothes between shifts. Ore shipments were transported in sealed boxes and protected by armed guards. In one instance, one carload of ore alone was worth $1 million. The overhead tram was improved, running from the vaulted doors of the Cresson to Elkton. The Cresson Mine quickly became the second largest producing mine in the history of the district. Richard Roelofs and the Harbecks stood back and smiled. A lot. Stockholders back in Chicago smiled also, especially when million-dollar dividends were distributed to them in 1915. Roelofs himself eventually retired to New York City, where he lived very comfortably to the age of 80.

The Cresson Mine had given the Cripple Creek District the boost it needed. Writer Julian Street, however, did not. In 1914, Street caused a commotion when his travel article for *Colliers Magazine* consisted entirely of his impressions of Myers Avenue in Cripple Creek. Among other things, Street noted some crib doors with the names Clara, Louise, and Lina on them. "I walked up the main street a little way, turned off and ran into Myers Avenue, the old red light street, with a vacant tumble-down dance hall and a long line of tiny box-stall houses called "cribs." Street's column included an interview with 43-year-old Mrs. Leola Ahrens, better known as Madam Leo.

Back in more prosperous times, Madam Leo had once stood, naked and drunk, on the corner of Fourth and Myers shouting, "I'm Leo the Lion, the queen of the row!" She was also credited with running prostitute Lillian Powers out of town at the turn of the century. When Street met her, however, Leo was a subdued middle-aged woman with "jet black hair and orchid colored cheeks." She also appeared to be a half-wit. Later, Street commented on his infamous article further. "I had not intended to write about Cripple Creek but the depressing place and the woman made such an impression on me that I described it in *Collier's Weekly*, for which the series was written."

Street went on to describe how furious the city of Cripple Creek was, including their barrage of letters to both himself and *Collier's*. On top of it, several newspapers published editorials about Street's offense. It was even said that the Cripple Creek city council voted to change the name of Myers Avenue to Julian Street, although there is no evidence to support that claim. The threat made the Associated Press wire services and was broadcast across the nation. Street's interview with Madam Leo likely did little to improve her status in the dying boom town. It certainly did nothing for Street's reputation in Cripple Creek.

A "vug" at the Cresson Mine gave the failing district a brief reprieve. For Richard Roelofs, an employee of the mine for many years, the find guaranteed his fame in Colorado history annals. (Courtesy Cripple Creek District Museum.)

118

9. END OF AN ERA AND THE SAVING OF CRIPPLE CREEK (1915–1960)

When Bert Carlton purchased the Cresson Mine for $4 million, his generosity seemed to take on a shine all its own during the Cripple Creek District's final bonanza. Other of Carlton's benevolent acts included repurchasing the failing Colorado Trading and Transfer Company, as well as buying the Midland Terminal Railroad. Like so many, Bert was hoping for a revival of the gold boom. It didn't happen, but Carlton continued his efforts for several years.

During World War I, while the nation in general struggled through a recession, Cripple Creek was about the only community to continue to thrive both economically and socially, but Prohibition and the Flu Epidemic of 1918 did little to enhance the district's fading glory. Production in the mines dropped significantly as gold prices fell. Only the Cresson remained a major producer, even after the station house below the Elkton mine closed in 1919 and a major recession hit the nation in the aftermath of World War I. By the 1920s, farmers, ranchers, miners, and others in and around the district were struggling to survive.

Once again, the local papers had little to report on, other than Ku Klux Klan activities in Canon City and the premiere of automobiles on the streets of Cripple Creek. Fire raised its ugly head again in September 1920, when the Victor Opera House burned. At the time, the opera house was said to be the largest structure in the Cripple Creek District and had played host to many famous performers. Built at an original cost of $65,000, the building was a total loss estimated at $100,000. The opera house's owner, E.H. Hall of Denver, was insured for no more than $6,500, which was not enough to replace even the impressive $7,000 organ. The opera house was never rebuilt.

But there was yet another industry to be discovered, that of guest ranches and skiing. In 1924, pioneer Don Lawrie recalled the ranch his folks had owned in the declining town of Midland between Divide and Cripple Creek. Measuring 160 acres per the Homestead Act, the Lawries called their place the Fig Leaf Ranch. Lawrie's parents "Sunny Jim" and "Lady (Jessie) Lawrie" reigned supreme, offering log cabins, well-balanced meals, horses, and stocked fish ponds. The price was 50¢ for a bed and 50¢ per meal.

Like the rest of America, the stock market crash of 1929, the Depression, and the Dust Bowl of the 1930s did much to facilitate the district's eventual downward spiral. Bert and Ethel Carlton finally gave up on many of their investments in the district and took an apartment at the five-star Broadmoor Hotel in Colorado Springs. Bert died in 1931. By then, most of the district's once flourishing towns were downsized to populations of just one or two families. Cripple Creek was sinking fast and, from the rest of the world's view, was on the edge of becoming a ghost town.

A number of people, however, still held the district dear to their hearts. They included pioneer families, as well as tourists who decided to make the district their permanent home. Certain that the mines of the district would one day boom again, local residents struggled for ideas to bring Cripple Creek and its surrounding cities back to life. Thus, when some local businessmen came up with the unique idea of staging a donkey derby in 1931, everyone thought it was a great idea.

From Montana to Kansas to California, historic mining towns have found new life based on their claims to fame. Each offers a myriad of historic buildings and attractions that draw thousands of visitors each year. Some, like Tombstone and Dodge City, feed from their reckless pasts. Still others, including Colorado's own Leadville, have maintained steady tourism simply based on their historic

The Imperial is seen here shortly after the Mackins bought it. Even today, the Imperial Hotel is the only continuously operating hotel in Cripple Creek. (Cripple Creek District Museum.)

Today, most passing motorists barely notice what little is left of Midland. The town once aspired to be a major stop along the Midland Terminal Railroad, complete with a fancy depot and a classy hotel.

charm. In Cripple Creek's case, the city opted to honor their own moving historic landmarks—descendants of donkeys used in the mines some decades ago. During the district's heyday, donkeys were as important to the mines as any modern day piece of mining machinery. These sturdy little animals could haul ore, pull wagons, and serve as valuable pack animals. Their use was so common that many were even born underground, living and working in the hundreds of tunnels comprising the mines.

When the mines played out and the miners left, they left their donkeys behind. Over time, the herd worked its way into the flower beds, garbage cans, and hearts of local residents. They made special friends of generations of children, housewives, and business owners, who gave them pet names and fed them. Posing with a beloved four-legged friend was a favored pastime among shutter-bugs. The number of offspring each year was something to talk about. People delighted in bribing them with food in order to pet their rough hides and stroke their big soft ears.

Beginning in 1931, Donkey Derby Days was established to honor these hard worked animals and boost tourism at the same time. According to legend, a man named Lynch, who managed the Palace Drug Store in Cripple Creek, first came up with the idea of Donkey Derby Days. In an effort to promote tourism in the district, Lynch suggested to buddies Charley Lehew and Bryan Jones that they hold a donkey derby. A racecourse was laid out and plans were made for snack booths and entertainment. Art Tremayne, who was born in 1917 and came to the district as a child, participated in the first Donkey Derby in August of 1931. The first race, according to Tremayne, ran from the Imperial Hotel at Third Street

The opening of the Carlton Tunnel in 1941 gave miners and mine owners hope, if only for a little while. (Courtesy Cripple Creek District Museum.)

and Bennett to where the Butte Opera House is just past Second and Bennett. "I didn't do very good," Tremayne recalled of his first race. "I had a donkey who was stubborn."

Founders of that first Donkey Derby Days decided to donate their proceeds to help other organizations. One of the first recipients was Canon City, which was able to open a talking movie theater with funds donated from the event. Within a year of the first donkey derby, the Two Mile High Club was formed to care for and feed the donkeys. With the club's help, each annual donkey derby made the herd more legendary. Today, Donkey Derby Days is celebrated each June and features races, parades, and many other exciting events.

During 1932, President Franklin D. Roosevelt's New Deal led to an increase in mining. No matter what the state of the economy, gold was still a viable product. During those years, the Works Project Administration and the Civilian Conservation Corps worked to maintain roads and bridges in Phantom Canyon, as well as other county roads. Roosevelt's efforts to put the nation back on its feet caught on in Cripple Creek, especially in 1935 when Roosevelt requested Congress to set the price of gold at $35 per ounce. Compared to the average $20 per ounce that had prevailed since the beginning of the district's boom, the price increase was the saving grace for many miners. By the end of 1935, annual production of gold in the Cripple Creek District was back up to $4.5 million.

Plagued by continual flooding problems, mine owners once more coordinated the building of another drainage tunnel. In 1939, the Carlton Tunnel was built with money from Bert Carlton's estate, contributed by his family and friends after his death. Not only did the new tunnel solve once and for all the drainage problems in district mines, but water from the tunnel also provided irrigation for Colorado's eastern plains. Construction was completed in 1941, and the Carlton Tunnel is still in use today.

World War II took as much of a toll on the Cripple Creek District as it did on other parts of United States. The war caused mining operations to slow or be suspended all over the country. While mining more practical minerals such as copper increased, gold mining fell. The Cresson Mine was one of only a few mines to continue operating during this period. By May of 1943, nearly all the mines in the district had closed. At the end of World War II, however, a good number of mines were able to reopen and the Carlton estate decided to build a new mill between Victor and Cripple Creek.

The reopening of the mines coincided, however, with the discontinuation of the Midland Terminal Railroad to the Cripple Creek District. For years, the railroad had been suffering and even Bert Carlton could not save it. The closing of the railroad was indeed a historic event with several former employees, as well as Ralph Carr and Lowell Thomas, boarding the train for its last run. Local radio stations and the *Colorado Springs Gazette Telegraph* provided extensive coverage of the event.

Despite the closing of the railroad, several other major events occurred in the late 1940s and 1950s to convert the district into a tourist destination. Mining endeavors may have been on the decline, but people who loved the district and its fascinating history refused to give up. Between established residents of the

Former Colorado Governor Ralph Carr (standing) and world traveler Lowell Thomas (seated to the right of Carr) were among those to ride the last Midland Terminal train to Cripple Creek in 1949. (Courtesy Cripple Creek District Museum.)

district and a handful of newcomers, the population managed to stick together and create a true sense of community. One of the best known newcomers to make a difference in the revival of Cripple Creek was Jack Schwab. A native of South Dakota, Schwab arrived in Cripple Creek sometime before World War II. Schwab later enjoyed telling of how on his first night in Cripple Creek, he unknowingly camped directly below a sewer outlet on the banks of the actual Cripple Creek. "That was the shittiest cup of coffee I ever had," he would later say.

Those who knew Jack said he was outspoken, brash, and one of the most influential people in town. In about 1945, Jack and his first wife Evelyn purchased a building along Bennett Avenue and christened it the Cottage Inn. Venison dinners, choice entrees, and alcohol figured prominently on the menu. And there was illegal gambling to be had. Jack quickly teamed up with Bert Bergstrom. Born in Sweden in 1896, Bergstrom first migrated to the United States in about 1912 and eventually found his way to Cripple Creek. He opened the Cripple Creek Inn in 1934 and was the first in Teller County to procure a liquor license after Prohibition was repealed.

Between the two men, illegal gambling ran quite rampant in Cripple Creek. Jack had 15 to 20 slot machines, which he moved around in order to elude the law. He seemed to regard the law as a detriment to his business as much as authorities regarded him a criminal. Once, two FBI agents called him and demanded he come up to the courthouse for a talk about his illegal slot machines. Jack simply replied that it made as much sense for him to walk up there as it did for them to come to the restaurant and hung up the phone.

Jack and Evelyn Schwab's Cottage Inn, visible down Bennett Avenue on the right, livened up the dying boomtown of Cripple Creek. (Courtesy Cripple Creek District Museum.)

There was little doubt the authorities regarded Jack Schwab as a troublemaker. His pet monkey Alice was more of a nuisance than an attraction. He was known to let his horses run loose through town and never hesitated to brandish a gun when he thought it necessary. One night, he fired his gun in the direction of his friend Bob Weymire. "It's a good thing that damn thing wasn't loaded!" said Bob. "Sure it was," replied Jack. "Take a look at your hat." Weymire removed his hat and found a neat bullet hole through the top of it.

Another time, two women ordered dinner at the Cottage Inn, but after the soup and salad were served, they left without paying. Jack lit out after them, heading them off on the hill above town at gunpoint. The frightened tourists offered to pay for the meal. "When someone orders a meal at my joint, they eat it," Jack said. The women were accordingly escorted back to the Cottage Inn, where they ate—and paid for—their dinner. If the locals were entertained by Jack's antics, they fairly rolled with laughter the night a woman stopped in and demanded, "Just what do you get with the venison dinner?" Jack didn't miss a beat. "Well, mostly you get a good case of the shits," he replied bluntly.

For all of his no-nonsense, law-be-damned demeanor, however, Jack Schwab also performed several benevolent acts. When the St. Nicholas Hospital needed a new furnace room, Jack raised the money to build it himself. He also became a staunch promoter of Donkey Derby Days. When Jack died in 1961, he was buried at Mt. Pisgah Cemetery with his favorite watch and a quart of whiskey, Cripple Creek style.

There is little doubt that Jack Schwab made an impression on everyone he met. But other newcomers to Cripple Creek left an even longer lasting impression, such as Wayne and Dorothy Mackin of Colorado Springs. In 1946, the Mackins really got the ball rolling by purchasing the old Imperial Hotel on Third Street in Cripple Creek. Built in 1896 by M.J. Roseberry, the building originally served as an office building and later as part of a successful hotel. The building was flanked to the north by the Collins Hotel and to the south by the Pittsburg Building, which contained Shockey's Pharmacy.

About 1905, the Collins Hotel expanded into the Roseberry Block, which was re-christened the Collins Annex. Mrs. Mary E. Shoot, proprietress, worked hard to maintain the hotel's fine reputation. She also spared no expense in her advertising, although she did drop the room rates to start at $1 per day. Upon completing renovations in about 1910, Mary Shoot renamed the Collins the Hotel Imperial. Shoot wisely listed the hotel as both the Hotel Imperial and the Imperial Hotel. Because of this, the business was and continues to be known under both names.

Mary Shoot turned over management to George and Ursula Long of Denver in 1914. Ursula Long ran the stately hotel, while George appears to have preferred painting. The grand re-opening under the Longs' management on March 1, 1914 made headlines in Cripple Creek. "The house, newly decorated and furnished, is very attractive," reported the *Cripple Creek Times*. "The dining room, brilliantly lighted, and the tables laid with everything new, sparkling with slender vases filled with carnations on every table, made a very pretty sight."

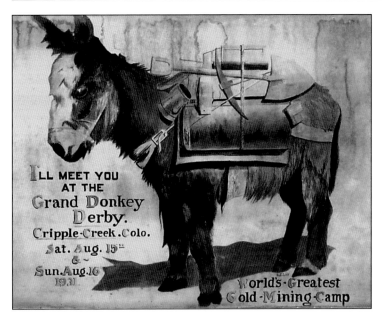

George Long painted the advertisement for the first Donkey Derby, which today is held at the Cripple Creek District Museum. Sometime in the 1950s or 1960s, the date of the celebrations was changed from August to the third weekend in June.

In keeping with the times, the refurbished hotel offered rates from $1 to $2.50 per day and its facilities continued to be upgraded over the next few years. Advertisements in 1916 offered American- and European-style lodging, modern conveniences, well-ventilated rooms, and a telephone. The Longs and their four children settled into a seemingly normal life. One woman recalled how, as a young unwed mother, she was taken in and given employment by Ursula Long. The women would lock the baby in one of the rooms, surrounded by pillows to prevent injuries, while they cleaned the hotel.

Although the spacious dining room closed in 1925, the Longs continued operating the hotel until the 1940s when George passed away. Ursula deemed caring for the old Collins too excessive for Cripple Creek's declining population and sold the original hotel to the YMCA. The Imperial Hotel stood empty until Wayne and Dorothy Mackin purchased the building. According to Dorothy, she and Wayne decided to purchase the Imperial in anticipation of gold prices escalating. Little did the couple dream their new enterprise would prove to be its own gold mine.

The Mackins set about creating a fine dining atmosphere and accommodations in the hotel, which quickly gained a good reputation with tourists and locals alike. When the Colorado Springs Chamber of Commerce booked a convention in 1947, they requested entertainment. The Mackins obliged by hiring the Piper Players, a melodrama crew from Idaho Springs. Dorothy would later write, "We . . . presented the first play in a corner of the dining room for the Chamber group. The following evening, we presented another performance to the Sylvanite Club . . . "

The stage was set. Realizing their potential for boosting tourism, the Mackins decided to build a theater in the basement of the old hotel. In June of 1948, the

Piper Players returned to Cripple Creek and it was they who worked alongside the entire Mackin family to make the dream come true. The end result was a cabaret-style theater with gaudy Victorian wall paper, beautiful red glass gooseneck lamps, and theater lighting, with furnishings fashioned from old brass and iron bedsteads. The Mackins purchased a piano with stained glass and an antique hotel sideboard to use as a back bar. An old fashioned theater curtain was painted into a mural advertising local and regional businesses. The overall design assured a good seat anywhere in the house. A former closet was converted into a stairway entrance and papered with canceled stock certificates from district mines.

Amazingly, the work was finished in just over a month. The Gold Bar Room Theater opened on July 3, 1948 with the Imperial Player's season premier of *Curse You Villain*. Soon, it was all the rage to attend the Imperial's Melodrama shows. Ethel Carlton, widow of Bert Carlton, attended often. Actors and celebrity guests were encouraged to sign little black top hats, hundreds of which adorned the room. Among the famous folks who visited the Gold Bar Room were Victor Borge, Walt Disney, Arthur Godfrey, Mary Tyler Moore, actress Lily Pons, astrologer Linda Goodman, Governors Ralph Carr and John Love, and Lowell Thomas. Craig T. Nelson, star of the television series *Coach*, once performed as an Imperial Player. His signature adorns a back hallway behind the theater alongside nearly every other performer in the Melodrama since its inception.

As Cripple Creek saw a resurgence of tourism, the Mackins saw their business increase more each year. In searching for new talent across the country, Wayne and

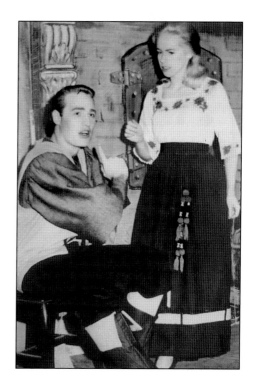

Actor Craig T. Nelson is among the hundreds of actors who have performed in the Melodrama. (Courtesy Mackin Collection, Cripple Creek District Museum.)

127

Dorothy also promoted Cripple Creek. Even today, the family deserves credit for boosting the economy during lean times. Their hard work paid off as more and more visitors began attending the Melodrama.

Mining also saw a brief resurgence. By 1951, $49 million in gold had been mined from the Cresson shaft, which dipped an astounding 2,400 feet below the surface. But although speculators knew there was still plenty of gold in the Cresson, it was still too expensive to mine. The nearby Mary McKinney mine closed in 1953 after producing $11 million in gold.

But there was still more new "gold" to be found in the Cripple Creek District. The success of both the Imperial Melodrama and Donkey Derby Days encouraged the opening of more tourist attractions. When a billboard was erected outside of Woodland Park, it depicted miner Rufus Porter, a.k.a. "the Hard Rock Miner" and "the Hard Rock Poet," pointing the way to the district. The painting included Porter's own beloved burro, Easu. Both Porter and Easu participated in Donkey Derby Days regularly, winning the race in 1952. Rufus went on to become a successful columnist for the *Colorado Springs Gazette Telegraph* and published several small booklets about the history of the district.

In 1953, the Cripple Creek District Museum premiered. Today, the museum's 50-year history is nearly as fascinating as the history inside it. It all started when Richard Johnson's one and only marriage ended and he came west. On the way

Rufus Porter and Easu are pointing the way to Cripple Creek, c. 1952. Porter, a.k.a. the Hard Rock Poet, published a number of books reminiscing about the district. During the 1960s, his colorful vignettes were also regularly featured in the Colorado Springs Gazette Telegraph. *(Courtesy Cripple Creek District Museum.)*

back from a trip to Las Vegas, Johnson stopped in Colorado Springs to see a friend, stage producer and millionaire heir Blevins Davis. As it happened, Davis was considering buying the *Cripple Creek Times & Victor Daily Record*, the only surviving newspaper in the Cripple Creek District. "Blevins asked me if I wanted to go into the publishing business, and I said yes," Johnson recalled. "So I came here to get a divorce and never went home."

The year was 1951. Dick Johnson, just 29 years old, had already seen a lot of life for such a young man. The son of a banker in Iowa, Johnson left home at age 17 to attend college first at the University of Minnesota and later at George Washington. After earning degrees in economics and philosophy, Johnson next applied for a job with the United Nations and was hired as head of civilian personnel for all of France.

After stints in Toronto and London, Johnson landed in Paris where he had both an apartment in the city and a home in the country, plus his own car and driver, and even a plane at his disposal. Such a prestigious lifestyle led to meeting an impressive variety of celebrities, largely through Johnson's friendship with Blevins Davis. And it was his longtime friendship with Davis that made a difference in Cripple Creek. Davis, ever curious to see what his investments might bring, bought the old Midland Terminal Depot and told Dick Johnson to start a museum. Then Davis left town.

Johnson obligingly spoke with several widows of Cripple Creek millionaires. By then, he was hobnobbing with the likes of Julie Penrose, Ethel Carlton, Mrs. E.W. Giddings, and other notable people who appreciated his sincerity. It also didn't hurt that Dick made quite a dashing figure and was unquestionably accepting of his friends' eccentricities. Once, Dick was visiting Mrs. Giddings at her home on North Cascade Avenue in Colorado Springs. The maid had the day off, so Mrs. Giddings simply called the five-star Broadmoor Hotel on the other side of town and ordered a pot of coffee to be brought over. "I have never turned on a gas stove," she told Johnson, "and I do not intend to start now."

With the financial backing of Mrs. Giddings and others, Dick Johnson created what is now among the oldest museums in the nation, the Cripple Creek District Museum. Upon his return, Blevins Davis repaid the loans. Johnson remembered that during the visit, Blevins also brought the Ballet Theater of America for a visit to Cripple Creek. At Jack Schwab's Cottage Inn, the entire troupe performed rodeo dances on top of the bar and tables to the music of the jukebox. "It was the prettiest performance I've ever seen," Johnson recalled.

With that, Blevins departed once again and left Johnson to revive Cripple Creek through both the museum and the newly christened *Gold Rush* newspaper. Johnson's work was balanced with time spent among Cripple Creek's social circles, which were the epitome of nouveau riche. Grand dinners, cocktail gatherings, and bridge parties were still the rage in Cripple Creek; black tie and formal dress the mode of the day.

At the museum, elderly pioneers seemed to come out of the woodwork to donate items from the district's incredible past. Today, the walls are lined with

Built by Spencer Penrose and Charles Tutt in 1918, the five-star Broadmoor Hotel in Colorado Springs became a refuge for many district millionaires.

rare photographs and documents pertaining to many of the 25 towns that once thrived within the district, and a number of rooms display life in the nineteenth and early twentieth century. On opening day in June 1953, Colorado Governor Dan Thornton himself spoke from the third-floor balcony. The Cripple Creek District Museum was open for business.

Although it was no longer economically feasible for most, mining became a popular hobby to many. People from out of town began buying homes in the district and using them as summer cabins. Throughout the 1950s, there were still several buildings standing at Elkton, Independence, Anaconda, Spring Creek, and other towns. Ghost town fever caught on as tourists began spending their vacations in the district, ratting around in the old mines and hiking in the hills. Such activities encouraged the establishment of the Victor Improvement Association in 1954. The organization was formed by a group of Victor women seeking to improve the quality of civic life in Victor. In about 1958, they also established the annual Gold Rush Days to celebrate Victor's mining heritage.

Over in Cripple Creek, efforts to revive the city were complete with the 1958 opening of the Old Homestead Parlor House Museum. The Old Homestead remains as the only survivor of several parlor houses that once lined Myers Avenue. This unique facet of the past was still intact on bawdy Myers Avenue, not far from where Julian Street conducted his infamous interview with Madam

Leo. Even today, the Old Homestead stands out as one of the only museums of its kind in the United States.

The Old Homestead may have opened as early as 1891, but little else is known about the brothel until 1896, when the place burned along with much of the red light district. At the time, the bordello was under the ownership of Isabelle Martin, better known as Pearl DeVere. The divine Ms. DeVere took out a loan and rebuilt her bordello to include such modern appliances as electric lights, running water, and even a telephone. Wallpaper was imported from Europe and the finest in furniture was installed. Pearl set high standards for her parlour house. Employees were expected to be classy and refined at all times.

For the gentleman who wished to visit the Old Homestead, there were prerequisites. To begin with, his reservation had to come with a $50 deposit. This was followed by a waiting period, during which the prospective customer's credit was checked. If the madam was satisfied with the man's financial background, she arranged an appointment with him. The Old Homestead charged $50 per "trick" or $250 for all night, the equivalent of the five tricks each girl was expected to turn per night.

Once inside, the gentleman was treated to the finest of food, liquor, and entertainment. Three parlors were provided for these purposes. Upstairs, a viewing closet allowed the customer to pick which girl he liked. The viewing room was a closet with a glass door, through which each girl passed for the customers' perusal. Customers were often assigned to the girls by Miss DeVere

Richard Johnson was just 29 years old when he first laid eyes on Cripple Creek. (Courtesy Richard Johnson.)

herself. From the viewing closet, the newly joined couple usually proceeded to one of five upstairs bedrooms.

The infamous Madam DeVere met her end at the Old Homestead in 1897 from a morphine overdose. Hers is the most well-remembered funeral in Cripple Creek history. Much of the town turned out to salute the charitable painted lady, whose donations to the poor and help to the sick were not soon forgotten. The funeral procession turned right onto Bennett Avenue, complete with a brass band, soiled doves, and mournful admirers. The Old Homestead continued operating in various capacities and some old-timers maintain the brothel was in business as late as the 1930s or 1940s. Following its closure, the Old Homestead became a boarding house and later a private home. When Pat and Fred Mentzer purchased it in the 1950s, the couple decided to renovate the house to its original splendor and opened it as a museum in 1958.

The opening of the Old Homestead, combined with the District Museum and the Imperial, did much to boost the economy of Cripple Creek. The Imperial installed a buffet service in their restaurant in 1959. Donkey Derby Days was running strong. Art Tremayne recalled when one of his favorite donkeys, a jack named Sam, won the Derby during the mid-1960s. Another famed four-legged friend won the race three or four years in a row and gave Cripple Creek the prestigious title of "Donkey Capital of the World." Mining, however, continued to suffer. Even at $35 per ounce, gold was too expensive to mine underground.

Today, the Old Homestead is one of the only brothel museums in the United States. A tour gives visitors much information about life at the Homestead, including period furnishings, fixtures, and photos of some of the girls who worked there. (Courtesy Cripple Creek District Museum.)

10. STRUGGLES AS A TOURIST MECCA (1960s–1980s)

As the Cripple Creek District melded into its new status as Colorado's largest "ghost" district, the area actually became rampant with history buffs and treasure hunters. Brian Levine, Caroline Bancroft, Cathleen Norman, Kathi MacIver, Leland Feitz, Linda Wommack, Mabel Barbee Lee, Muriel Sybil Wolle, Perry Eberhart, Ray Drake, Robert L. Brown, and Tom Noel are just some of the many writers to record the history of the Cripple Creek District for the pleasure of tourists, history buffs, and genealogists.

Residents of the district were beginning to truly capitalize on the district's fantastic history. The Victor Improvement Association, which had formed in 1954, officially incorporated in 1960 and set about creating a new museum in Victor. Local volunteers, donations, and services helped make this dream a reality. The old Reynolds Block on the corner of Third and Victor Avenue was purchased and renovated. With the help of locals who donated an array of memorabilia, as well as the estates of Lowell Thomas, Charles Tutt, and Ethel Carlton, the museum opened in about 1961. The Victor Museum was not without its problems; a failing economy and a boiler that exploded in the museum made for difficulties. Even so, the museum set a precedence for Victor's tourism potential, as well as that of the district.

The year 1961 also saw the arrival of Bill Robinson, who purchased the *Gold Rush* newspaper from Dick Johnson. In his time, Robinson played a prominent role in Donkey Derby Days and the further promotion of the district. He is credited with rejuvenating the failing Two Mile High Club and also served as mayor of Cripple Creek for several years. "He was the best mayor I remember," said Dick Johnson. Even so, Robinson's efforts were often criticized by his opponents in small-town politics. "He was so used to criticism," recalled Johnson. "Once I tried to compliment him on the smoothly paved streets and he got mad. He thought I was being sarcastic. He said 'You S.O.B., if you don't like it why don't you just move?' "

Politics or not, the abandoned roads, buildings, and mines of the district were mighty inviting to visitors who could get a last glimpse of life in a boom camp.

Mollie Kathleen Gortner refused to listen to foolish men who told her she could not stake her own claim. It was said that women were unlucky in mines; whenever Mollie visited her own operation, her employees came to the surface immediately and respectfully waited for her to leave before resuming their work. (Courtesy Mollie Kathleen Gold Mine.)

Most of the mines were open and quite dangerous; outside of Anaconda, the Mary McKinney Mine's huge cribbing paralleled the highway and frightened tourists who dared to drive past it. But part of the thrill came in exploring the ghost towns of the Cripple Creek District. Visitors enjoyed poking about in the abandoned homes at Elkton, Independence, Altman, and Mound City where furniture, refuse of yesteryear, and personal belongings still lay scattered about.

In response to the growing number of visitors and newcomers who yearned to taste a piece of the district's history first hand, the Mollie Kathleen Mine above Cripple Creek opened for tours. A real and continuously operating mine since 1891, the mine owed its fame to Mollie Kathleen Gortner, who persuaded her husband Henry to move to the district when the couple's son Perry gained employment as a surveyor in the area. On a trip up Poverty Gulch to look for elk, Mollie chanced to find the same type of "float" that had so intrigued Bob Womack some years earlier.

When Mollie showed her find to Perry, he lost no time in sitting on the claim while his mother hurried to the claims office. It is said that Mollie was immediately turned away, simply because she was a woman, and that she reacted by grabbing the claim papers and signing them anyway. "My Henry is an attorney," she informed the surprised man at the desk, "and you can argue with him when he arrives from Colorado City." Thus, Mollie Kathleen Gortner became the first woman in the Cripple Creek District to stake a mining claim and name it after herself.

The Mollie Kathleen experienced continuous success, riding the ups and downs with the rest of the district for decades. When Mollie passed away in 1917, Henry followed shortly thereafter and Perry was left a one-third interest in the mine. Perry continued operations until his death in 1949. By 1961, when the Carlton Mill was closed down, tourists had already been a familiar sight at the Mollie Kathleen for some time. Rather than close the mine, the owners opted to continue operating it as a tourist attraction. Even today, the Mollie Kathleen is the only gold mine tour to feature a vertical shaft (at a depth of 1,050 feet) in the United States.

And more was coming. The year 1964 saw the arrival of Lodie and Harold Hern from New Mexico. The couple purchased Jack Schwab's Cottage Inn on Bennett Avenue and carried on Jack's reputation for fine food and libations. Then in 1967, the Cripple Creek & Victor (CC&V) Narrow Gauge Railroad in Cripple Creek opened as the dream-child of John Birmingham, whose fond memories of train rides as a child stayed with him into adulthood. Birmingham had purchased some narrow gauge engines in 1965 and decided to build his own railroad. The ideal location turned out to be in Cripple Creek, where the grades from the defunct Midland Terminal Railroad were still very much accessible.

Construction on the railroad began in June of 1967, next door to the Cripple Creek District Museum. Birmingham utilized former railroad workers and

The Cripple Creek & Victor Narrow Gauge Railroad opened in 1965 to give tourists a taste of railroading from the old days. (Courtesy Dow Helmers Collection, Cripple Creek District Museum.)

train buffs to assist in the project and established connections to gather needed materials and advice on how to proceed. By the end of the year, Cripple Creek's newest attraction was taking visitors up and down a 1-mile stretch of track. In 1968, Birmingham purchased the old Midland Terminal station from nearby Bull Hill and moved it to Cripple Creek.

Within two more years, the CC&V Narrow Gauge Railroad reached the ghost town of Anaconda, 4 miles away. Engineers along the ride relished telling tales about the history of the district. From the tracks, visitors were (and still are) treated to bird's-eye views of Cripple Creek and the district's back country with its historic mine headframes and abandoned buildings, as well as glimpses of the spectacular Sangre de Cristo mountain range to the south. Today, the trip dead-ends at the old blacksmith barn for the Mary McKinney Mine, one of the few relics left in Anaconda.

As visitors to the district learned its history, certain residents were still making a history of their own. One of the last celebrity figures to take an interest in the district was astrologer Linda Goodman, who moved to Cripple Creek in 1968. A successful author known for her eccentricities, Goodman spread good will throughout her time in Cripple Creek. Many of her well-known books were written here.

Prior to her arrival in Cripple Creek, Linda Goodman had run like the ultimate wild child through the fancy restaurants and elegant homes of New York and California. Born and raised in West Virginia, Goodman had an enriched childhood. "Linda had advantages," related her best friend Evelyn Stauffer in 1995. "She would pay the neighbor kids not to step on ants." Thus began the life of a compassionate humanitarian. After beginning a career in journalism, Linda's talent quickly escalated to include play writing, radio, and eventually astrology. By the time she migrated to Cripple Creek, she was already the successful author of *Linda Goodman's Sun Signs*, a startlingly accurate account describing each sign of the zodiac. Four more books were written during the 1970s and 1980s, and each work illustrates Goodman's remarkable grasp of the astrological world.

From all accounts, Linda Goodman burst with intelligence while appearing insane, or at least eccentric, to the outside world. The people in her life were at her beck and call, her whim and fancy. They were loved, they were wanted—at her leisure. She spread her generosity like great gossamer wings, encircling those she cared about with an iron-like grip. Loyalty won her heart. "She had that star quality," said longtime friend Dick Johnson. "She was kind of far out, but I always thought she was very intelligent. She dominated every group she was in, whether people liked her or not."

Stories of Goodman's eccentricities are still abundant in Cripple Creek. There was the time she stepped behind the counter at the grocery store and began tearing up *Playboy* magazines. One day, a couple of locals found her stumbling up from Myers Avenue, babbling about getting caught in a time warp and fighting with a prostitute. For years, she continued to set a place at the dinner table for her daughter Sally, an aspiring actress who allegedly died in 1970. She

World-famous astrologer Linda Goodman made her home in Cripple Creek and mentioned the city often in her books. Even today, longtime fans come to Cripple Creek to see the famed author's stomping grounds.

also erected a chapel in her home dedicated to Mannu, a religion she founded that combined the teachings of her personal saint, St. Francis of Assisi, and Native American beliefs.

While residents of Cripple Creek may have questioned Linda Goodman's sanity, there was clarity and sense in her writing. Many of her books are collector's items today. And despite her reckless reputation, most who knew Linda loved her with a passion. She grieved in her own way over the loss of four of her seven children. Her generosity became well known, driving her to the point of bankruptcy several times. At Dick Johnson's antique store in Cripple Creek, she often purchased jewelry to pass out as tips around town. "Linda walked to a different drummer. She was a marvelous lady," recalled Katherine Hartz, another close friend of several years.

Bob Lays, formerly of the Palace Hotel knew Linda for several years. It wasn't until a young fan of Linda's approached him, however, that Bob realized her fame. The lady wanted to meet the author. Bob called Linda, who bought lunch for the trio. Lays also recalls Linda treating large groups of friends to dinner at the Palace. She favored the same table and tipped the waitstaff well. Close friends were invited to Linda's home to view *Gone with the Wind* and another of her favorite movies, *Brother Son Sister Moon*. Actors Barbra Streisand and Christopher Reeves were among her personal heroes.

Harold and Lodi Hern purchased the Cottage Inn and the Old Homestead Museum, while Harold worked as principal of the school at Cripple Creek. (Courtesy Harold and Lodi Hern.)

But for all her generosity, Linda Goodman also had a sinister side. "She was a very moody person and could be stern," Lays remembered. "She wanted her way." Some regarded Linda's refusal to see fans as rude. She was in the habit of answering the door to strangers under the guise of a secretary and telling them Linda Goodman was unavailable. "She loved her fans, but she didn't want to be bugged by them," said Evelyn Stauffer. The woman who had dined with the likes of Howard Hughes, Marilyn Monroe, and John F. Kennedy was like any celebrity, striving to keep her personal life personal.

Evelyn Stauffer was Linda's closest companion during the last years of her life. The two met at a restaurant in 1989, when Evelyn casually informed some inquiring tourists that Linda was out of town while the famed author dined at a nearby table. Evelyn's trust was gained and the two became close friends. They began spending a lot of time together. Linda delighted in purchasing identical outfits for the two of them to wear. Linda's infatuation with twins led her to encourage Evelyn to become her likeness.

Instead, Evelyn became Linda's constant companion. With utmost loyalty, Stauffer tolerated her friend's eccentricities and did what she asked, often spending the night at her home. "If I didn't wake her up in the morning to tell her I was leaving, she became furious with me." With time, Linda worried about people who might take advantage of her. Evelyn was always there to soothe her fears. "I loved her. She was a wonderful, wonderful person," Evelyn said. "She taught me a lot. I don't regret one thing about being her friend." Linda died in 1995, but even today her fans continue to visit Cripple Creek and inquire about her.

By 1969, the Cripple Creek District ranked among the top visitor's spots in Colorado. Retail shops abounded, as well as attractions like the Cripple Creek & Narrow Gauge Railroad and the Mollie Kathleen Mine. The Imperial Melodrama had become nationally famous. Harold and Lodi Hern expanded their business interests and purchased the Old Homestead Museum, as well as a former "colored" brothel that they converted into the Red Lantern Inn. Harold, who served as the principal at Cripple Creek's school from 1966 to 1987, was tickled at being the only school employee "to own a whorehouse and a bar." Over the next several years, the Red Lantern became known as the place where many locals preferred to eat and drink.

Then, in approximately 1971, the old Cresson Mine was purchased by the Cripple Creek and Victor Gold Mining Company. The new conglomerate resumed drawing the precious metal from the earth and expanded its operations to include Arequa Gulch and a myriad of mountains. In 1974, President Richard Nixon removed Franklin Roosevelt's $35 per ounce cap on the price of gold and the price rose dramatically. Following Nixon's decree, further underground exploration and the processing of waste dumps escalated into the 1980s.

Some say that singer John Denver further helped increase the interest in Colorado's heritage and beautiful natural resources during the 1970s. Denver's wistful folk tunes, especially his number one hit "Rocky Mountain High," brought about a new appreciation for Colorado and the bountiful forests, history, and scenic drives the state had to offer. Denver's success, combined

Henry "June" and Margaret Hack (middle) both grew up in the Cripple Creek District. Pictured with them are Arlia McManus with her granddaughter (both on left) and Janice Wood of the Gold Camp Victorian Society (right).

with a resurgence in mining, affected the Cripple Creek District in a positive way, boosting the economy even more. People like the Lays of the Palace Hotel and others were enticed to buy property in the historic district and try their luck at tourism.

Unfortunately, the end of the 1970s was marked by the loss of the Grubstake Hotel and June and Margaret Hack's grocery store at the corner of Second and Bennett Avenues in Cripple Creek due to a fire. In his younger days, Henry "June" Hack made the papers often as one of the best young boxers in the region. He met Margaret, the daughter of area pioneers, at the Victor Elks Lodge and the two have been married for over 50 years as of this writing. For 25 years, the Hacks ran their grocery store, where the district's famous herd of wild donkeys were a familiar sight.

In March of 1977, a fire of unknown origins erupted at the Grubstake Hotel, located in what had been known as the Welty Block. Formerly, the 50-room building had housed Cripple Creek's Masonic Hall. As flames engulfed the building, the fire departments of both Cripple Creek and Victor fought the blaze against such odds as frozen fire hydrants and frigid temperatures. As in the fires of 1896, dynamite was ultimately used to blow up one wall and stop the flames. But the loss was still quite large, including the Welty Block in its entirety and the Hack's grocery store next door.

The Lowell Thomas Museum opened as the Victor Museum in 1961. Contained in two buildings featuring four floors and several rooms, the museum aspires to be one of the best museums in the state.

Interestingly, one of dozens of ghost stories about Cripple Creek surfaced in the wake of the Welty Block fire. When the back wall collapsed, a spiraling column of flames shot upward as at least two firemen heard a woman's screams from inside the empty building. One of them was volunteer Ed Grosh, who swore he heard a woman's voice calling out, "I'm free! I'm free at last!" In the years since the fire, more and more stories have emerged about the old Welty Block being haunted before its demise. Some even swore they saw the apparition of a woman floating through the smoke. As for June Hack, all he saw after the fire were four donkeys, standing at the burned out door of his grocery and looking at the ruins with quizzical expressions. "That fire devastated us and them," he said.

The 1980s signified the loss of several well-known citizens who had done much to save the Cripple Creek District. Following the death of Lowell Thomas in 1981, the Victor Museum board of directors renamed the institution the Lowell Thomas Museum in his honor. Lowell's heirs reciprocated the gesture by paying for an exterior paint job and a salaried curator, as well as a gift of $15,000 worth of stock in CBS. The trustees later sold the stock to finance a new roof and foundation repairs.

Thomas's death did more than boost tourism for his namesake museum. People in general began to realize the value of talking to old-timers who could remember area history. Some, such as Ohrt Yeager of Victor, were virtual blasts from the past. For some 50 years, Ohrt served as the owner of Zeke's Place, one of Victor's last authentic watering holes. Zeke's served a number of locals, but also visitors from out of the area who stopped by the tavern on a regular basis. Sitting at the old scarred-up bar that ran forever down one side of the room, one could watch a slice of the world that others rarely saw. The place was filled with nicotine-stained bar signs and the infamous nude portrait of Marilyn Monroe had a prominent place above the mirrored back bar. Miniature draft horses on the Budweiser display silently pulled a tiny beer wagon in circles.

Most memorable to many was a vintage photo of Ohrt Yeager, which smiled out over his magic and funky little kingdom. Born to a farmer in Longmont, Ohrt's family lost everything in the Depression. That's when the family came to Victor, in about 1934, to pursue mining. When Ohrt returned from serving in World War II, he joined the Elks Lodge and settled in for good. Shortly after the Yeager's moved to Victor, Ohrt's father bought Zeke's from its original owner, Zeke Bennett. Most locals firmly agree Zeke's opened in 1893. While Ohrt toiled in such well-known mines as the Ajax and the El Paso, his dad worked to build Zeke's into the hearty little bar it was when Ohrt took it over in the 1960s.

In between telling his tales, Ohrt served his famous chili. Other times, as customers sat and chatted, Ohrt shuffled around the bar, appearing to strangers as no more than a clean-cut janitor, with a white starched shirt and suspenders. In about 1989, Ohrt went away due to health problems from working in the mines. When he reappeared, he was toting an oxygen tank, but was just as spry as ever.

Only one slight dilemma arose as Ohrt's employees often became preoccupied with keeping Ohrt and his oxygen tank from getting too near the tiny little grill.

Nothing could keep Ohrt from stirring his chili or whipping up one his incredibly good burgers. Ohrt finally retired to Florence, Colorado and passed away in 2001. Unfortunately, Zeke's closed in 2002, even though Ohrt's famous chili was being served at the Pepsi Center arena in Denver.

One last matriarch to fall in the 1980s who bears mention is Gertrude Dial, the great-aunt of rock musician Stevie Nicks. Dial was born Gertrude May Neppel in 1912, near what is now Evergreen Station in the Four Mile District. It was Gertrude's brother Ed who partnered with Jacob Abby at the district dairy town of Spring Creek. Ed likely attended the wedding of his sister Gertrude to a miner named Benjamin F. Coffin in 1928. The two were married in Colorado Springs, but the Coffin family first appeared in the district back in 1896. The union was short-lived; Ben Coffin's death in 1934 happened to coincide with the opening of Bert Bergstrom's Cripple Creek Inn on Bennett Avenue in Cripple Creek. When Bert moved to Woodland Park in 1945, the CCI, as it was known, fell into the hands of Gertrude and her second husband Ralph "Speed" Dial.

For about 20 years, Gertrude and Speed ran the Cripple Creek Inn. Gertrude also ran The Girl's Café in a building along South Second Street, purchased the old Palace Hotel with her sister Maud Playford, and ran a boardinghouse in the old Bell Brothers Building across from the courthouse. After Speed Dial passed away in 1970, Gertrude next ran several successful antique shops in Cripple Creek. It is said that her famous niece, Stevie Nicks, visited her often on clandestine trips to the district. Even today, residents recall meeting or seeing Ms. Nicks on several occasions. The celebrity is a legend in her own right in the district, with stories ranging from arriving in town in a limo to attending parties at Victor's old Gold Coin Club.

Gertrude died in 1989 and her ashes were spread on a nearby mountaintop. As far as anyone knows, Stevie Nicks has not graced the district with her presence since. She did leave behind one curious salute to Cripple Creek, however—if the story is really true. It is said that Nicks's song "The Imperial Hotel" from her 1983 *Wild at Heart* album is dedicated to Cripple Creek's own historic landmark.

11. ELEVEN YEARS OF GAMING (1991–2002)

Cripple Creek is experiencing its third era of gaming. The first occurred with the founding of Cripple Creek and the district surrounding it in 1891. Gambling was rampant in the Cripple Creek District; despite being illegal, gaming houses and saloons ran day and night. Many of these were located on Bennett Avenue in buildings that are still standing today. Of the original gambling halls, Johnny Nolon's Saloon and Gambling Emporium is the only one to continue business under its original name and at its original location.

Although gambling amused many a miner and millionaire, it was not the pastime future generations have come to know. Slot machines were a very minor facet of the gambling world. What existed in their stead were games like Roulette, Craps, Poker, and Faro, a very fast and popular game laid out on a board with numberless cards. The Faro dealer whose hands could fly over the cards and count money quickly was a well-paid and respected man. The game was also very easy to cheat at, however, which is why we never see it played today.

The first Cripple Creek District Directory was published in 1893. Already, many "sampling rooms," saloons, and clubs were listed in Cripple Creek. They included Anheuser-Busch at 416 Bennett Avenue, Becker & Nolon at Bennett and Third, T.R. Lorimer at 225 Bennett, and the Turf Sample and Club Rooms at 219 Bennett. Nearby towns also listed several dance halls, sample rooms, and saloons. The 1896 Cripple Creek City Directory shows 76 saloons, all of which offered gambling. Gambling also extended itself to certain brothels such as The Old Homestead. Gaming rooms began competing for business. The Lorimer Block included electric lights, hand-blown drinking glasses, and cards at the ready on every table. Elegant gambling parlors like Lorimer's and Johnny Nolon's, with its Brunswick pool tables, catered to the more elite and established social ranks for gamblers.

In the next four glorious years, money swirled around Cripple Creek like snowflakes. Everyone was making money and gambling reached an all-time high as an acceptable sport. Surrounding towns were well off too. Gillett, with its fine racetrack and casino just 4 miles away, was a popular resort. In nearby Victor, miners toiled by day, gambling and drinking their wages away by night. Stories

During Cripple Creek's first era of gambling, such sinful paraphernalia as poker tables and faro boards were burned in front of the Teller County Courthouse. (Courtesy Cripple Creek District Museum.)

of divorce and desertion peppered the newspapers on a regular basis. Hence, by 1900, attitudes toward gambling were changing. The district had perhaps become too wild and a little too carefree. To start with, many citizens felt affronted by the whirring sounds of roulette wheels and slot machines spilling onto the streets as they passed down Bennett. Just the sight of an actual betting game in progress was viewed as offensive. Then came the arrival of the Women's Christian Temperance Union (WCTU), comprised mostly of angry wives who were tired of watching their families go hungry due to the demon gambling.

The WCTU was a very elite social group that had actually been striking terror in the hearts of gamblers, prostitutes, and drinking men for some time. The WCTU was anti-gambling, anti-drinking, anti-everything that seemed fun. Their members made it their mission to make it "hot" for gamblers and saloon owners until the latter gave in and either quit their antics or left town. By 1900, the WCTU had successfully shut down gambling in Leadville and Denver before making a beeline for Cripple Creek. Within a short time, nickel slots were outlawed in the district. City officials also prohibited poker tables and roulette wheels on the first floor of any establishment. Regardless of the fuss, Cripple Creek still sported 64 saloons, many of which included a number of poker parlors.

One establishment seemed to suffer less discomfort than others in the wave of anti-gambling. The Newport Gambling Hall was located in the southwest corner of the first floor of the Mining Exchange Building. Many a rich executive found his way to the Newport, run by Grant Crumley. A former gang member and exfaro dealer, Crumley's reputation was well known in Cripple Creek. But even the Newport had little protection from theft. Grant's roulette table was robbed at least twice by armed, masked men in 1900. Other incidents seemed to echo the WCTU's visit. One Mary J. Cassady won a longtime lawsuit against John Nolon in 1900. Mrs. Cassady claimed that back in 1894, her husband had gambled away $6,000 of her own money at Johnny Nolon's saloon. The suit was finally settled for $4,000 in Cassady's favor. The WCTU had also affected town merchants and many large saloons who wanted gambling closed down.

The death of Sam Strong, gold mining magnate, seemed to punctuate gambling problems in 1901. Sam had run up a gambling tab of $2,500 at the Newport, which he paid by check. The next day, Strong stopped the check, claiming the roulette wheel was fixed. A week later, Strong settled with Grant Crumley for $200. All seemed well until one night when Sam and some friends ambled into the Newport. Strong was very drunk and jeered at Crumley, even when he managed to win $140. At the bar, there was a brief exchange of words before Strong suddenly withdrew a revolver. He shouted at Crumley to take his hands from his pockets. Crumley reacted by pulling a sawed-off shotgun from under the bar. In the next moment, Strong lay on the floor, a puddle of blood slowly spreading around his head. He died a few hours later, and Crumley was acquitted of the killing. Grant Crumley's actions put one cap in Sam Strong and another cap on the first gambling era of Cripple Creek. In 1902, the city officially outlawed

This photograph of Sam Strong lying on the floor of the Newport was actually posed by Strong supporters days after his death. (Courtesy Ray Drake Collection, Cripple Creek District Museum.)

145

gambling. Shortly afterward, Crumley, Johnny Nolon, and other gambling kings in town closed up shop and moved on to other destinations.

But gambling in Cripple Creek never quite faded. In 1903, the ever-popular private men's clubs were reprised, and not surprisingly, these clubs allowed poker. Men who could not afford the expensive membership dues could still participate in one of several illicit games taking place in the back rooms of the district. Raids were made at sporadic intervals over the next decade, often to little avail. As late as 1913, Police Chief Nolan caught five men gambling in Victor. Eventually, gambling dwindled to no more than a friendly card game at the bar or in somebody's kitchen. The roulette wheels disappeared and the card tables were converted for other uses. Slowly but surely, the saloons and gaming houses of Cripple Creek evolved into ice cream parlors, restaurants, or novelty shops, while their owners worked to conform or simply left town.

What gambling devices were left in the district were altered to dispense gum and other sundries. Only a few places, like the Home Café and the Elk's Club, kept slots around as a so-called novelty. Soon, however, it became obvious that certain of those "display" slot machines were serving the same old purpose. The new laws were ignored by those who could not resist the roll of the dice or a wild

After opening the Cripple Creek Inn in 1934, Bert Bergstrom later moved to Woodland Park's Ute Inn. Within a few years, Bert was leading parades—and the town. (Courtesy Ralph White, Ute Inn.)

These slot machines were donated to the Cripple Creek District Museum by Cripple Creek BPOE #316 in the 1960s.

poker game. For decades, many a card game was broken up by police, who hauled the offenders off to jail and confiscated the dreaded gambling paraphernalia. From Cripple Creek to Victor, through Florissant and Woodland Park, and even down Ute Pass, the die-hard gambler could find a game if he knew where to look. For nearly half a century, gambling conducted itself in a clandestine manner for those who dared to break the law.

As late as 1951, three major gambling raids took place in Woodland Park. In all three cases, the spirit of gambling and the underworld showed itself in uncanny ways. Bert Bergstrom was found not guilty for running slot machines at the Ute Inn, due to lack of evidence. Lorin Chamberlain was tried after someone saw him carrying two slot machines into the Wrangler Inn. The key witness admitted to playing slot machines in Woodland Park, but could not identify those two particular slot machines as ones he had played. But the best story lies with the Thunderhead Inn with its Vegas showgirls, an establishment that was closed after gambling was discovered in a nearby cabin. A truck carrying the confiscated equipment broke down and was left sitting on the road overnight. Come morning, the roulette wheel, chips, dice, and cards were mysteriously missing, taken back no doubt by their original owners.

Talk of gambling ceased with time, but somehow the players always found a way to maintain their pleasurable pastimes. Even throughout the 1970s, the illegal games continued, making the occasional headline when the law had nothing better going on than breaking them up. Finally, by the 1980s, gambling was all but gone in Teller County. The Cripple Creek District was still relying heavily on the tourist season. Then in about 1989, the Little Ike Tunnel on Highway 67 suffered a small cave-in requiring big repairs. As the district appealed to the state to fix the tunnel and the state in turn laid the burden on the county, tourism took a dramatic downswing. Visitors, especially those from out of state, were laboring under the misconception that there was no other way to access the district.

That's when the folks in Cripple Creek began paying close attention to what Central City, a failing boomtown in Gilpin County west of Denver, was considering. Central City and its neighboring town of Blackhawk were talking about legalizing limited stakes gambling within their city limits in order to boost their economies while preserving their pasts. Encouraged by stories of how gambling had revitalized the town of Deadwood, South Dakota, a group of local business owners decided to get on the bandwagon and join Central City and Blackhawk's efforts. Campaign literature explained that 50 percent of all gaming proceeds would go to the Colorado General Fund, with another 28 percent providing historic preservation funding statewide. In addition, Teller and Gilpin Counties would net 12 percent, with the last 10 percent being distributed among the cities of Cripple Creek, Central City, and Blackhawk.

In Cripple Creek, the campaign effort was spearheaded by Harold and Lodi Hern; Terry Wahrer, who had purchased the Red Lantern in 1983; Bob Konczak, who owned Johnny Nolon's old building; and Ted Mueller, president of the Cripple Creek Bank. Other local business owners, including Jim Minow, Bill Fox, Ted Roell, Candy Hopp, June Hack, and Bob and Marcy Hepner also joined in. Together, the group hired a lobbyist by the name of Freda Poundstone to do their bidding at the state capitol in Denver. Poundstone's fee was a phenomenal $200,000, consisting of $10,000 investments from several interested parties. In addition, the petitioners were required to pay $1 per signature, with 100,000 signatures required, in order to get the gambling initiative on the ballot. "A lot of people thought we were out of our minds in our effort to get gambling in Cripple Creek," Harold Hern recalled, "but gambling did pass."

Indeed, in November of 1990, Colorado voters approved limited gaming in Cripple Creek, Central City, and Blackhawk by an amazing 68 percent of the vote. Interestingly, this is the only time gambling has ever been made officially legal in Cripple Creek. At the Cripple Creek Elks Lodge, Harold Hern estimated that as many as 600 people gathered round to hear the results on election night. Afterward, he remembered, "It was one hell of a party."

Opening day was set for October 1, 1991. During the months preceding that historic date, Cripple Creek became a flurry of realtors and construction crews. Current building owners were scrutinizing their old structures and trying to visualize what was to come. Diane and Jon Zimmer were among those to prepare ahead, renovating the Phenix Block. Prior to the new construction, the Phenix was no more than a dilapidated facade with no back wall, floors, or roof. When finished, the Phenix made quite the presence on Bennett Avenue and was a good example of what could be done with an old building.

Other buildings received face lifts as real estate prices sky-rocketed. Many historic buildings were gutted, their antique fixtures and woodwork sold or thrown out like so much garbage and replaced with new floors, ceilings, and walls. Contemporary Victorian decor quickly became the mode of the day as most casino owners hurried to prepare their gaming houses for the thousands of gamblers that were sure to come.

The first casinos to officially open on October 1, 1991 were the Black Diamond, the Brass Ass, Bronco Billy's, Creeker's, Johnny Nolon's, the Narrow Gauge, and the Phenix House. The next day saw the premier of Cripple Creek's Ore House, followed by the Colorado Grande on October 10, the Silver Mine on the October 12, Wild Bill's on October 16, and the Turf Club on October 20. In their wake, both the ghosts and the locals of Cripple Creek must have surely been awakened by the thundering of thousands of feet traversing the streets for the first time in decades.

The first years of gaming in Cripple Creek were wild. The city was a virtual sea of people and money moving deftly from one casino to the next. Music poured into the streets as the crowds mingled within the historic buildings. With all the free coupons flying around, it was said that a person could walk up one end of Bennett and down the other getting free coins, free meals, and free drinks, and still come out ahead without ever touching a slot machine.

In the air above it all, there was nearly an audible vibration as the city came to terms with what could be called the second great gold boom in its 100-year-old

Seven casinos opened with legalized gambling at Cripple Creek on October 1, 1991. Today, approximately 15 casinos intermingle with shops, arcades, and museums.

The Cripple Creek and Victor Mine employs an average of 300 workers and has produced over 1 million ounces of gold. At this time, the mine is predicting no less than another ten years of strip mining before its operations in the area are complete.

life. Now as then, money flew around like autumn leaves in a grove of aspen trees. For the first time in Colorado, employees could expect hourly wages well above their counterparts in non-gaming cities. Bartenders, waitresses, and dealers had every right to be upset if they got off work with less than $100 in tips in their pockets. Everybody was happy, it seemed, and everybody was making money and having fun.

Gambling also brought an amazing series of physical changes to the Cripple Creek District. A large percentage of the population, many of whom had struggled financially for years, took the chance to sell their commercial buildings at a hefty profit. With the prospect of untold millions of dollars in income looming on the horizon, everybody wanted to get in on the game. Differences of ideas, opinions, and ethics made for one interesting melting pot of folks who all had a plan in mind for reasons both good and bad. Thus, Cripple Creek has seen its share of heroes and villains with one common goal: make Cripple Creek boom.

And boom it has, with a sound audible all the way to Denver. Sometimes, the boom has come in the form of a wrecking ball. Other times, the boom has been merely the sound of hammers on nails as buildings are renovated, reconstructed, or built under new construction. Still other times, the boom has been heard over the hills at the nearby Cripple Creek and Victor Mine, whose 1980s expansions of the historic Cresson Mine now reach far beyond what any miner imagined a century ago. If Richard Roelofs were standing at the shaft today, along with Eugene and J.R. Harbeck, the three would be proud to know their worthless little mine is still producing millions.

The Little Ike Tunnel at Waters is closed but still intact. Longtime visitors to the district recall the day when they had to drive into the one-way tunnel to make sure no one was coming from the other way before proceeding.

The overall facelift has been amazing. Even locals who have lived here all their lives have a hard time recalling where everything was and what has changed. Most of the district's historic ghost towns have been buried or razed by the mine. In the political arena in Cripple Creek, however, eyebrows soon began to raise at the idea of demolishing historic buildings. Still, what was a charming ghost town to visitors was being viewed as an eyesore by others. Gaming was here and it was time to catch up with the rest of the world. In 1993, highway travelers were both relieved and alarmed when Highway 67 was built around the Little Ike Tunnel. As a historic landmark of the Colorado Midland Railroad, the one-lane tunnel had caused traffic stress for years. Although it is now closed to all traffic, the Little Ike remains preserved with an interpretive sign about its history.

Perhaps the saving of the Little Ike Tunnel fueled the preservation fire in Cripple Creek, which by now had been brewing for some time. When an 1898 attorney's office on Second Street was threatened for demolition in the wake of a casino, city authorities were urged by both the state and the National Trust to take a more cautious approach. Longtime historian and preservationist Brian Levine was making his opinions heard loud and clear. Subsequently, the attorney's office was saved from destruction, as well as the Bell Brothers Building and three historic boarding houses on Carr Avenue.

Levine himself was appointed historic preservation director for Cripple Creek. Much like its appointee, the position was challenging and often controversial. During Levine's reign, the city managed to facilitate some new construction, such as the Double Eagle and Glitter Gulch casinos. More importantly, historic preservation funds were used for extensive renovations on the Bell Brothers Building (now the Cripple Creek Police Department), city hall, and the 1893 Colorado Trading and Transfer Building.

In the time since Levine left, Cripple Creek has seen even more changes, including a new school around 1997 and the complete reconstruction of the Butte Opera House. These benevolent projects have been countered by more than a few demolitions, but thankfully, there are still hundreds of historic buildings intact throughout town. Many of them even have their original interiors still intact, such as the Cripple Creek District Museum, the Elks Lodge, the Cripple Creek Hotel (formerly the high school), and the Teller County Courthouse. Both the Palace and the Imperial still sport their original hotel lobbies.

In addition, the Old Homestead remains untouched since its opening day as a museum back in 1958. In 1995, however, exorbitant taxes forced Harold and Lodi Hern to sell the Old Homestead to National Lodging, which owned the Jubilee Casino next door. When the Jubilee closed in 1998, the staff worked quickly to form the Old Homestead House Museum Inc. and vowed to purchase the structure. In the time since, the Old Homestead has been closed off and on, reopening under new rallies of support and with the inception of the annual "Pearl's Follies." Ironically, this is a family event wherein local residents pool their talents to put on a rollicking variety show. The museum still offers tours year round, publicizing their needs through Pearl's Follies and other fundraisers.

Other on-going traditions include the Imperial Melodrama. As of 1996, the Melodrama was the oldest continuously running melodrama in the United States. Dorothy Mackin liked to boast that there was never one cancellation under the their management—rain, snow, or shine. Then the sound of hearts breaking was nearly audible when Dorothy Mackin passed away and the shows discontinued

The historic Bell Brothers Building is one of several that have been renovated with historic preservation funds since gambling was legalized. (Courtesy Cripple Creek District Museum.)

Dorothy and Wayne Mackin played a major role in the revival of Cripple Creek. Their purchase and subsequent opening of the old Imperial Hotel was a sign of better things to come, plus some of the finest dining and accommodations Cripple Creek had seen in quite some time. (Courtesy Steve and Bonnie Mackin.)

after years of continuous performance. Following the demise of the Melodrama at the Imperial, several national acts appeared at the Gold Bar Room before it was closed by the fire department around 1998. Even today, however, the Imperial is working diligently to bring the old theater up to code and open it once more. In the meantime, the Melodrama found a new home at the renovated Butte Opera House beginning in 2000. The shows are still produced by the Mackin family and continue to offer the traditional Melodrama entertainment so many have come to love.

As with any boom, the wild days have smoothed out in time. Nowadays, nationwide gambling has a firm grasp on Americans, most of whom know the ins and outs of the activity. Veteran gamblers are a common sight and most casinos now have established routines that seldom leave room for doubt on the part of customers or employees. Gambling today has taken on a clean, resort-oriented atmosphere, and the rumble of Carrie Nation as she rolls over in her grave is audible no more.

With $5 maximum stakes, Cripple Creek offers gaming in a historic and small-town atmosphere. The town currently boasts about 12 casinos, each with its own distinct personality and amenities. Of these, seven in-house hotels accompany the numerous lodging facilities and bed-and-breakfast inns around the district. Most

Cripple Creek continues to host several popular events throughout the year. Some, like Donkey Derby Days, are decades-old traditions.

casinos have restaurants, from complimentary hot dog stands and snack bars to casual and fine dining. Operating hours of the majority of the casinos in Cripple Creek run from 8 a.m. to 2 a.m. seven days a week, year round. The gaming allure is still as prominent as it was ten years ago, and combines nicely to make Cripple Creek a well-rounded town that combines a variety of attractions for families and gamblers alike.

The casinos complement Cripple Creek's numerous city-wide events and retail shops that pepper the downtown district. Because nobody under the age of 21 is allowed on the gaming floors, Cripple Creek briefly lost its reputation as a family destination. But thanks to efforts by city officials, commercial property owners, private individuals, and the casinos themselves, Cripple Creek is re-emerging as the "kids of all ages" resort it has always been. Visitors to the district today can enjoy gambling as well as a variety of museums, attractions, the Melodrama, hiking trails, horseback riding, and other activities.

In addition, Cripple Creek's donkey herd still consists of about a dozen well cared for and spoiled creatures. Over the years, new donkeys have been occasionally combined with the original herd to bring fresh blood and prevent birth defects. It is almost certain, however, that there is a touch of their true historic ancestors in each one. Unlike a building that stays in one place, the donkeys' favorite hobby is roaming. They can be found most anywhere, at any time, which makes finding them all the more fun. In 2002, sculptor Michael Slancik completed his latest project, "The Locals." The bronze sculpture depicts a mother and baby donkey, and has a prominent place in front of the Cripple Creek District Museum.

It is true, the changes in Cripple Creek have brought with them some interesting ramifications. A trip to nearby Victor, however, gives visitors a good idea of what Cripple Creek was like before gaming. The Fortune Club at Victor Avenue and Third Street has retained much of its original flavor and offers the best malts anywhere on the planet. The Lowell Thomas Museum across the street offers even more historical information and walking into the Victor Elks Lodge is like passing through a time warp.

Many of the buildings of Victor remain virtually untouched. Of special interest are the Masonic Hall and the *Victor Daily Record* building, located in close proximity to one another on Fourth Street. The Cripple Creek and Victor Mining Company, which has to date milled over 1 million ounces of gold, has done much to assist in the renovation of other buildings. In 2000, the mine poured concrete sidewalks for the Lowell Thomas Museum and rebuilt the west side foundation. In addition, a historic preservation consultant was hired to oversee the upgrading of the exhibits. The company has also hired college students to keep the museum open in the summers.

Just beyond Victor is the town of Goldfield, whose quiet neighborhoods reflect the essence of mountain living. The city hall continues to be under renovation. Although commercial businesses have not flourished in Goldfield for decades, the

Despite the absence of a business district, Goldfield survives as a thriving bedroom community. During the 1980s, the Cripple Creek District Museum assisted in the purchase of the city hall, which has since been restored.

district's third largest—and only other surviving—town still retains its old-time feel. For the most part, Goldfield continues to survive as somewhat of a bedroom community, with many original homes kept up among a number of decaying buildings and a handful of modern dwellings.

True to their original intent, Colorado casinos pay device fees and taxes that continue to go to the state for disbursement of historical grants and preservation efforts. A large number of historic buildings all over the state have benefitted from gaming, finding new life as museums, schools, and commercial endeavors. In addition, Cripple Creek and the district around it have found new life and renewed economies unlike anything they have seen in nearly 80 years. Gambling and gold: these are the two assets the Cripple Creek District has always had, and will continue to have, for decades and generations to come.

These are the district's moving landmarks. Today, descendants of the donkeys used in the mines a century ago still wander the streets of Cripple Creek.

BIBLIOGRAPHY

Author unknown. "Florence R.R. History." Unpublished manuscript, date unknown. From the collection of Jan MacKell.

Bauer, William H., James L. Ozment, and John H. Willard. *Colorado Post Offices 1859–1989*. Golden, CO: Colorado Railroad Historical Foundation, 1990.

Brown, Robert L. *Colorado Ghost Towns*. Caldwell, ID: The Caxton Printers, Ltd., 1972.

———. *Ghost Towns of the Colorado Rockies*. Caldwell, ID: The Caxton Printers, Ltd., 1968.

Calhoun, W.C. "History of Cripple Creek, America's Famous Gold Camp." *The Quarterly Sentinel*. Vol. I, No. 1. February 1896: 1–5.

Chronic, John and Halka. "Prairie Peak & Plateau, A Guide to the Geology of Colorado." *Colorado Geological Survey Bulletin 32* (1972): 57–61.

Cornell, Virginia. *Doc Susie*. New York: Random House, Inc., 1991.

Cripple Creek District Directories, 1893–1918.

Cripple Creek District Museum. *Official Cripple Creek Up to Date, 1896*. Cripple Creek, 1896.

Denver City Directory, 1892.

Eberhart, Perry. *Guide to the Colorado Ghost Towns and Mining Camps*. Chicago: Swallow Press/Ohio University Press, 1959.

Emrich, David. Hollywood, Colorado. Lakewood, CO: Lost Modern Company, 1997.

Feitz, Leland. *Cripple Creek Railroads*. Colorado Springs, CO: Little London Press, 1968.

———. *Victor, A Quick History*. Colorado Springs, CO: Little London Press, 1969.

Fetter, Rosemary. "Lowell Thomas: A Victor Legend." *The Colorado Gambler Magazine*. 22 January to 28 January 2002: 18.

"A Guide to the Hornbek Homestead at Florissant Fossil Beds National Monument." Published by Florissant Fossil Beds National Monument, Florissant, Colorado.

Hughes, J. Donald. *American Indians in Colorado*. Denver, CO: University of Denver, Department of History, 1977.

Jameson, Elizabeth. *All That Glitters*. Chicago: Board of Trustees of the University of Illinois, 1998.

Levine, Brian. *Cripple Creek: City of Influence*. Historic Preservation Department, City of Cripple Creek, 1994.

Lewis, Allan C. *The Florence & Cripple Creek Railroad*. Denver, CO: Sundance Publishers, 2001.

McFarland, Edward M. *The Cripple Creek Road*. Boulder, CO: Pruett Publishing Co., 1984.

Mehls, Steven F. and Carol D. *Goin' Up To Cripple Creek*. Prepared for the Gold Belt Tour Scenic and Historic Byways Association, Inc. and the Bureau of Land Management, Canon City Field Office. Bureau of Land Management, May 2001.

Ormes, Robert M. *Tracking Ghost Railroads in Colorado*. Colorado Springs, CO: Green Light Graphics, 1992.

Perlman, Dr. Selig. *History of Labor in the United States, 1896–1932, Volume IV, Labor Movements*. New York: Macmillan Co., 1935.

Pettit, Jan. *Ute Pass, A Quick History*. Colorado Springs, CO: Little London Press, 1979.

———. *Utes, The Mountain People*. Colorado Springs, CO: Century One Press, 1982.

Smits, Angel Strong. "Sam Strong: Cripple Creek's Notorious Millionaire." *Wild West Magazine*. August 2001: 39–42.

Spell, Leslie Doyle. *Forgotten Men of Cripple Creek*. Denver: Big Mountain Press, 1959.

Sprague, Marshall. *Money Mountain*. Lincoln, NE: University of Nebraska Press, 1953.

Stephens, Autumn. *Wild Women*. Emeryville, CA: Conari Press, 1992.

Taylor, Jean and Ann Cott. *A Century in the Shadow of Pikes Peak: Don Laurie, His Mountain, His Life*. Pueblo, CO: PaperWork Inc. , 1999.

Victor Centennial Committee. *Victor Centennial 1893–1993 Commemorative Book*. Victor, CO: Poco Libro Press, 1993.

Voynick, Stephen M. *Colorado Rockhounding*. Missoula, MT: Mountain Press Publishing Co., 1994.

NEWSPAPERS

Chicago Times

Colorado Springs Gazette

Cripple Creek Gold Rush

Cripple Creek Times

Denver Post

Rocky Mountain News

Victor Record

INTERVIEWS

Bumgarner, Charlotte

Hack, Henry and Margaret

Hern, Harold and Lodi

Hilliard, Stephanie

Johnson, Richard

Johnson, Sally McCready

Kane, Steve

McCormick, David

Swanson, Erik

Tremayne, Art and Loretta

Twitty, Eric

INDEX